IMMIGRATION IN THE 21
POLITICAL, SOCIAL AND E

IMMIGRATION INSPECTIONS AND ENFORCEMENT AT AND BETWEEN PORTS OF ENTRY

IMMIGRATION IN THE 21ST CENTURY: POLITICAL, SOCIAL AND ECONOMIC ISSUES

Additional books in this series can be found on Nova's website under the Series tab.

Additional e-books in this series can be found on Nova's website under the e-book tab.

IMMIGRATION IN THE 21ST CENTURY:
POLITICAL, SOCIAL AND ECONOMIC ISSUES

IMMIGRATION INSPECTIONS AND ENFORCEMENT AT AND BETWEEN PORTS OF ENTRY

MARCELLA MAGDALENA
EDITOR

New York

Library of Congress Cataloging-in-Publication Data

ISBN: 978-1-63117-409-4

Published by Nova Science Publishers, Inc. † New York

CONTENTS

Preface   **vii**

Chapter 1   Border Security: Immigration Inspections
at Port of Entry
Lisa Seghetti   **1**

Chapter 2   Border Security: Immigration Enforcement
between Ports of Entry
Marc R. Rosenblum   **49**

Index   **107**

PREFACE

Controlling admissions is a core element of state sovereignty, but such control entails the opposing goals of preventing unlawful entries, while facilitating legal flows. These policy goals are inherently in tension, as efforts to identify and interdict illegal entrants inevitably challenges, and may delay, the smooth flow of legitimate travelers. The Supreme Court has long held that Congress has absolute authority to control immigration by establishing rules for the admission, exclusion, and deportation of non-citizens. Thus, while the specific issues in U.S. immigration law have evolved over time, a core policy goal has always been to prevent the entry of aliens who threaten U.S. interests. This book focuses on discussing the inspections conducted at each port of entry and then continues to examine the enforcement of immigration between ports of entry.

Chapter 1 – About 362 million travelers (citizens and non-citizens) entered the United States in FY2013, including about 102 million air passengers and crew, 18 million sea passengers and crew, and 242 million incoming land travelers. At the same time about 205,000 aliens were denied admission at ports of entry (POEs); and about 24,000 persons were arrested at POEs on criminal warrants. (Not all persons arrested are denied admission, including because some are U.S. citizens). Within the Department of Homeland Security (DHS), U.S. Customs and Border Protection's (CBP) Office of Field Operations (OFO) is responsible for conducting immigration inspections at America's 329 POEs. CBP's primary immigration enforcement mission at ports of entry is to confirm that travelers are eligible to enter the United States and to exclude inadmissible aliens. Yet strict enforcement is in tension with a second core mission: to facilitate the flow of lawful travelers, who are the vast majority of persons seeking admission. A fundamental question for Congress and DHS is how to balance these competing concerns.

In general, DHS and CBP rely on "risk management" to strike this balance. One part of the risk management strategy is to conduct screening at multiple points in the immigration process, beginning well before travelers arrive at U.S. POEs. DHS and other departments involved in the inspections process use a number of screening tools to distinguish between known, low-risk travelers and lesser-known, higher-risk travelers. Low-risk travelers may be eligible for expedited admissions processing, while higher-risk travelers are usually subject to more extensive secondary inspections. As part of its dual mission, and in support of its broader mandate to manage the U.S. immigration system, DHS also is responsible for implementing an electronic entry-exit system at POEs. Congress required DHS' predecessor to develop an entry-exit system beginning in 1996, but the implementation of a fully automated, biometric system has proven to be an elusive goal. The current system collects and stores *biographic* entry data (e.g., name, date of birth, travel history) from almost all non-citizens entering the United States, but only collects *biometric* data (e.g., fingerprints and digital photographs) from non-citizens entering at air or seaports, and from a subset of land travelers that excludes most Mexican and Canadian visitors. With respect to exit data, the current system relies on information sharing agreements with air and sea carriers and with Canada to collect *biographic* data from air and sea travelers and from certain non-citizens exiting through northern border land ports; but the system does not collect data from persons exiting by southern border land ports and does not collect any *biometric* exit data. Questions also have been raised about DHS' ability to use existing entry-exit data to identify and apprehend visa overstayers. The inspections process and entry-exit system may raise a number of questions for Congress, including in the context of the ongoing debate about immigration reform. What is the scope of illegal migration through ports of entry, and how can Congress and DHS minimize illegal flows without unduly slowing legal travel? Congress may consider steps to enhance POE personnel and infrastructure and to expand trusted travel programs. Congress also may continue to seek the completion of the entry-exit system, a program that has been the subject of ongoing legislative activity since 1996, as summarized in the appendix to this report.

Chapter 2 – Border enforcement is a core element of the Department of Homeland Security's (DHS's) effort to control unauthorized migration, with the U.S. Border Patrol (USBP) within the Bureau of Customs and Border Protection (CBP) as the lead agency along most of the border. Border enforcement has been an ongoing subject of congressional interest since the 1970s, when illegal immigration to the United States first registered as a serious national problem; and border security has received additional attention in the years since the terrorist attacks of 2001. Since the 1990s, migration control at the border has been guided by a strategy of "prevention through deterrence"—the idea that the concentration of personnel, infrastructure, and surveillance technology along heavily trafficked regions of the border will discourage unauthorized aliens from attempting to enter the United States. Since 2005, CBP has attempted to discourage repeat entries and disrupt migrant smuggling networks by imposing tougher penalties against certain unauthorized aliens, a set of policies eventually described as "enforcement with consequences." Most people apprehended at the Southwest border are now subject to "high consequence" enforcement outcomes. Across a variety of indicators, the United States has substantially expanded border enforcement resources over the last three decades. Particularly since 2001, such increases include border security appropriations, personnel, fencing and infrastructure, and surveillance technology. The Border Patrol collects data on several different border enforcement outcomes; and this report describes trends in border apprehensions, recidivism, and estimated got aways and turn backs. Yet none of these existing data are designed to measure illegal border flows or the degree to which the border is secured. Thus, the report also describes methods for estimating illegal border flows based on enforcement data and migrant surveys. Drawing on multiple data sources, the report suggests conclusions about the state of border security. Robust investments at the border were not associated with reduced illegal inflows during the 1980s and 1990s, but a range of evidence suggests a substantial drop in illegal inflows in 2007-2011, followed by a slight rise in 2012. Enforcement, along with the economic downturn in the United States, likely contributed to the drop in unauthorized migration, though the precise share of the decline attributable to enforcement is unknown. Enhanced border enforcement also may have contributed to a number of secondary costs and benefits. To the extent that border enforcement successfully deters illegal entries, such enforcement may reduce border-area violence and migrant deaths, protect fragile border ecosystems, and improve the quality of life in border communities. But to the extent that aliens are not deterred, the concentration of enforcement resources on the border may increase border area violence and migrant deaths, encourage unauthorized migrants to find new ways to enter illegally and to remain in the United States for longer periods of time, damage border ecosystems, harm border-area businesses and the quality of life in border communities, and strain U.S. relations with Mexico and Canada.

In: Immigration Inspections and Enforcement ...   ISBN: 978-1-63117-409-4
Editor: Marcella Magdalena   © 2014 Nova Science Publishers, Inc.

Chapter 1

BORDER SECURITY: IMMIGRATION INSPECTIONS AT PORT OF ENTRY[*]

Lisa Seghetti

SUMMARY

About 362 million travelers (citizens and non-citizens) entered the United States in FY2013, including about 102 million air passengers and crew, 18 million sea passengers and crew, and 242 million incoming land travelers. At the same time about 205,000 aliens were denied admission at ports of entry (POEs); and about 24,000 persons were arrested at POEs on criminal warrants. (Not all persons arrested are denied admission, including because some are U.S. citizens.)

Within the Department of Homeland Security (DHS), U.S. Customs and Border Protection's (CBP) Office of Field Operations (OFO) is responsible for conducting immigration inspections at America's 329 POEs. CBP's primary immigration enforcement mission at ports of entry is to confirm that travelers are eligible to enter the United States and to exclude inadmissible aliens. Yet strict enforcement is in tension with a second core mission: to facilitate the flow of lawful travelers, who are the vast majority of persons seeking admission. A fundamental question for Congress and DHS is how to balance these competing concerns.

---

[*] This is an edited, reformatted and augmented version of Congressional Research Service Publication, No. R43356, dated January 9, 2014.

In general, DHS and CBP rely on "risk management" to strike this balance. One part of the risk management strategy is to conduct screening at multiple points in the immigration process, beginning well before travelers arrive at U.S. POEs. DHS and other departments involved in the inspections process use a number of screening tools to distinguish between known, low-risk travelers and lesser-known, higher-risk travelers. Low-risk travelers may be eligible for expedited admissions processing, while higher-risk travelers are usually subject to more extensive secondary inspections.

As part of its dual mission, and in support of its broader mandate to manage the U.S. immigration system, DHS also is responsible for implementing an electronic entry-exit system at POEs. Congress required DHS' predecessor to develop an entry-exit system beginning in 1996, but the implementation of a fully automated, biometric system has proven to be an elusive goal. The current system collects and stores *biographic* entry data (e.g., name, date of birth, travel history) from almost all non-citizens entering the United States, but only collects *biometric* data (e.g., fingerprints and digital photographs) from non-citizens entering at air or seaports, and from a subset of land travelers that excludes most Mexican and Canadian visitors. With respect to exit data, the current system relies on information sharing agreements with air and sea carriers and with Canada to collect *biographic* data from air and sea travelers and from certain non-citizens exiting through northern border land ports; but the system does not collect data from persons exiting by southern border land ports and does not collect any *biometric* exit data. Questions also have been raised about DHS' ability to use existing entry-exit data to identify and apprehend visa overstayers.

The inspections process and entry-exit system may raise a number of questions for Congress, including in the context of the ongoing debate about immigration reform. What is the scope of illegal migration through ports of entry, and how can Congress and DHS minimize illegal flows without unduly slowing legal travel? Congress may consider steps to enhance POE personnel and infrastructure and to expand trusted travel programs. Congress also may continue to seek the completion of the entry-exit system, a program that has been the subject of ongoing legislative activity since 1996, as summarized in the appendix to this report.

INTRODUCTION

About 362 million travelers (citizens and non-citizens) entered the United States in FY2013, including about 102 million air passengers and crew, 18 million sea passengers and crew, and 242 million incoming land travelers. At the same time about 205,000 aliens were denied admission at ports of entry (POEs); and about 24,000 persons were arrested at POEs on outstanding criminal warrants.[1] (Not all persons arrested are denied admission, including because some are U.S. citizens.)

Within the Department of Homeland Security (DHS), U.S. Customs and Border Protection's (CBP) Office of Field Operations (OFO) is responsible for conducting immigration inspections at America's 329 POEs. About 21,775 CBP officers inspect travelers, agricultural products, and cargo at U.S. ports and abroad.[2] Most foreign nationals visiting the United States also are subject to some form of screening prior to their arrival at a POE, including when they apply for a nonimmigrant visa or to enter through the Visa Waiver Program,[3] and through CBP's screening of information provided by air and sea carriers.

CBP's primary immigration enforcement mission at ports of entry is to confirm that travelers are eligible to enter the United States and to exclude inadmissible aliens.[4] This mission is challenging because of the scope and complexity of immigration inflows: millions of travelers at hundreds of ports must be individually screened against dozens of rules governing who may or may not enter the country. Moreover, strict enforcement is in tension with a second core mission: to facilitate the flow of lawful travelers, who are the vast majority of persons seeking admission. A fundamental question for Congress and DHS is how to balance these competing concerns. The answer to this question varies across diverse geographic regions, different modes of travel, and in response to a constantly shifting landscape of potential threats and legal immigration flows.

As part of this dual mission, and in support of its broader mandate to manage the U.S. immigration system, DHS also is responsible for implementing an electronic entry-exit system at POEs. Congress required DHS' predecessor to develop an entry-exit system beginning in 1996,[5] but the implementation of a fully automated, biometric system has proven to be an elusive goal.

This report reviews the legislative history of immigration inspections requirements and the entry-exit system. The report then describes the implementation of these provisions, including pre-travel screening, primary and secondary inspections, trusted traveler programs, outbound enforcement, and the entry-exit system. The final section of the report identifies a number of issues for Congress related to immigration admissions and enforcement at POEs.

IMMIGRATION INSPECTIONS: POLICY GOALS

Controlling admissions is a core element of state sovereignty; but such control entails the opposing goals of: 1) preventing unlawful entries, while 2) facilitating legal flows. These policy goals are inherently in tension, as efforts to identify and interdict illegal entrants inevitably challenges, and may delay, the smooth flow of legitimate travelers.[6]

The Supreme Court has long held that Congress has absolute authority to control immigration by establishing rules for the admission, exclusion, and deportation of non-citizens.[7] Some of the first federal laws, the so-called Aliens and Seditions Acts of 1798, authorized the president to arrest and/or deport any alien who represented a danger to the United States.[8] And while Congress during most of the 19th century generally favored open admissions to the sparsely populated country, a series of laws beginning in 1875 excluded several classes of aliens, including criminals and prostitutes,[9] aliens from certain countries and regions,[10] anarchists,[11] communists,[12] and aliens engaged in espionage,[13] among others.

Thus, while the specific issues in U.S. immigration law have evolved over time, a core policy goal has always been to *prevent the entry of aliens who threaten U.S. interests.* For the last several decades, these threats, or enforcement priorities, have fallen within three broad categories:[14]

- **Unauthorized immigration**. Since 1980, the estimated unauthorized population in the United States has increased from about 2.5 million to about 11.7 million people.[15] Between one-third and one-half of these aliens are believed to have entered lawfully through a POE and over-stayed their visas.[16] An unknown proportion of illegal entrants also passed through POEs, either concealed in a vehicle or by using fraudulent documents. One enforcement priority at POEs, therefore, is to prevent these unlawful entries, and to identify visa overstayers.
- **Transnational crime**. CBP officers performing immigration inspections are the primary line of defense against certain illegal flows, including in particular most illegal drug flows other than marijuana.[17] Immigration inspectors also seek to arrest known smugglers and other criminals at POEs.
- **International terrorism**. National security concerns have loomed large in immigration policy in the years since the 2001 Al Qaeda attacks against the United States (the 9/11 attacks). All 19 of the 9/11 hijackers entered the United States *legally* through POEs, and

constraining terrorist travel is now recognized as a critical defense against certain types of terrorist attacks.[18]

Yet while most people would agree that terrorists, criminals, and immigration violators are appropriate enforcement targets, no consensus exists about how to *prioritize* these threats because the likelihood of each type of illegal entry is unknown, and because the potential consequences of these threats are subjective and difficult to measure. The likelihood of each of these threats occurring also varies by geography and mode of entry. For example, certain types of illegal migrants may be more likely to travel by bus or car across the southern border, smugglers may favor other distribution routes, and terrorists may be likely to reach the United States by air and/or at northern border POEs. Threat actors also may seek to counter enforcement efforts by adapting their behavior to avoid such patterns.[19]

Enforcement must be balanced by a second overarching goal: the facilitation of legal flows. With international tourism directly accounting for an estimated $186 billion in 2011 (about 1.2% of U.S. gross domestic product),[20] travel facilitation supports the U.S. economy. Smooth processing at POEs also streamlines travel for the tens of millions of U.S citizens returning from international trips each year, and may improve Americans' experiences abroad through reciprocal arrangements. In addition, immigration agents at POEs define visitors' first impressions of America and the U.S. government, and therefore play an important diplomatic role.

Enforcement and travel facilitation are fundamentally in tension because efforts to identify and interdict unlawful travelers tend to impede the flow of the entire admissions queue, and efforts to expedite the line may increase the risk that an illicit traveler is overlooked. Thus, in addition to questions about how to *prioritize* diverse threats, Congress and DHS must decide how to *balance* enforcement and facilitation. Is it better to admit one illegal actor, or to delay the admission of 1,000 lawful travelers? How should Congress and DHS weigh the benefits of more robust enforcement against the costs to commerce, privacy and civil liberties, and related concerns?

In an effort to reduce border wait times without compromising border security, CBP's response to these questions emphasizes "risk management." In general, risk management refers to a process for assessing the risks associated with potential threats and calibrating the enforcement response to the estimated gravity of the threat.[21] In the case of immigration inspections, risk management involves screening travelers at multiple points in the immigration process to distinguish between low- and high-risk travelers. Low-risk travelers may be eligible for expedited admissions processing through the Visa Waiver Program and/or trusted traveler programs, while higher-risk travelers may be subject to more extensive secondary inspections. Unauthorized migrants at POEs may be subject to expedited removal and other types of immigration enforcement (see "The Immigration Inspections Process").

LEGISLATIVE HISTORY

Inspections for Admission

The procedures governing inspections of persons applying for admission are described in 8 C.F.R. §235, which derives its authority from sections 101, 103, 215, 221, and 235 of the Immigration and National Act of 1952 (INA, P.L. 82-414), as amended. Under INA §215, in particular, both aliens and citizens are required to present appropriate entry documents, except as otherwise ordered by the president; and (pursuant to 8 C.F.R §235.1) only to enter through designated ports of entry.[22] INA §211 spells out additional documentary requirements for immigrant admissions. And INA §287 authorizes immigration officers, among other powers and pursuant to regulations, to interrogate any person believed to be an alien as to the person's right to enter or remain in the United States, and to arrest any alien attempting to enter the United States unlawfully.[23]

Prior to 2002, INA §103 made the Attorney General responsible for controlling U.S. borders and enforcing these laws. Pursuant to §§401- 403 of the Homeland Security Act of 2002 (HSA, P.L. 107-296), these responsibilities were transferred to DHS.[24] The INA also authorizes the consular processing system as part of the visa issuance process, giving State Department consular officers sole authority to issue visas to aliens seeking admission to the United States.[25] Section 428 of the HSA charged DHS with issuing regulations on visa issuances and authorized DHS personnel abroad to advise consular officers and to review and investigate visa applications; but the HSA left the State Department in charge of actual visa issuance (also see "Consular Reviews").[26]

Historically, U.S. citizens and most citizens of Canada and Bermuda entering the United States by land or sea from the Western Hemisphere were exempted from certain document requirements.[27] Following the 9/11 attacks, based on a recommendation by the National Commission on Terrorist Attacks upon the United States (the 9/11 Commission),[28] section 7209 of the

Intelligence Reform and Terrorism Prevention Act of 2004 (IRTPA, P.L. 108-458) directed DHS, in consultation with the Department of State (DOS), to develop a plan to require a passport or other secure document(s) for all travel into the United States by U.S. citizens and others. The resulting plan, known as the Western Hemisphere Travel Initiative, requires adult land and sea travelers entering the United States from within the hemisphere to present a passport or other secure document.[29]

Entry-Exit System: Legislative Requirements

Section 110 of the Illegal Immigration Reform and Immigrant Responsibility Act of 1996 (IIRIRA, P.L. 104-208, Div. C) required the Attorney General, within two years of enactment (i.e., by September 30, 1998), to develop an automated entry and exit control system that would collect records of alien arrivals and departures and allow the Attorney General through online searches to match such arrivals and departures and thereby identify nonimmigrant aliens who remain in the United States beyond the periods of their visas (i.e., visa overstayers). The bill also required the Attorney General to annually report to Congress on the number of visa overstayers and their countries of origin.

Congress has amended the system's requirements and deadlines on several occasions since then, including by adding an entry-exit requirement to legislation authorizing the Visa Waiver Program and by requiring that the entry-exit system to include biometric technology and to be fully interoperable with DOS and Department of Justice (DOJ) databases. See **Appendix A** for a full list of entry-exit legislation. Despite Congress's ongoing attention, however, the entry-exit system remains incompletely implemented (see "Entry-Exit System: Implementation").

Travel Facilitation

With the increased focus after 9/11 on national security during immigration screening, Congress has taken steps to ensure that DHS also focuses on travel facilitation. Section 302(b)(1) of the Enhanced Border Security and Visa Entry Reform Act of 2001 (EBSVERA, P.L. 107-173), for example, directed the departments to "utilize technologies that facilitate the lawful and efficient cross-border movement of commerce and persons without compromising the safety and security of the United States." In addition, §7209(k) of the IRTPA described congressional findings that "expediting the travel of previously screened and known travelers across the borders of the United States should be a high priority," including because it "can permit inspectors to better focus on terrorists attempting to enter the United States." The section directs DHS to develop and implement a registered traveler program for this purpose (also see "Trusted Traveler Programs"). IRTPA §7210 also amended INA §235A to require DHS to add 25 preinspection stations (up from 5 required under IIRIRA) and to locate such stations at locations that "would most effectively facilitate the travel of admissible aliens" in addition to reducing the arrival of inadmissible aliens, as in the original language (also see "Preclearance").

THE IMMIGRATION INSPECTIONS PROCESS

Travelers seeking to enter the United States go through one to three steps in the immigration inspection process. In the first step, prior to travel, most travelers who are not U.S. citizens or legal permanent residents (LPRs)[30] must apply for permission to enter the United States, by obtaining a visa at a U.S. consulate abroad or through the Visa Waiver Program. Air travelers are subject to additional screening prior to arrival (see "Pre-Travel Screening"). Second, all arriving travelers are subject to inspection (or preclearance) by a CBP officer prior to entering the United States (see "Primary Inspections"). Third, some passengers also may be selected through risk-based screening or at random for more intensive scrutiny (see "Secondary Inspections and Immigration Enforcement"). Participants in CBP's trusted traveler programs volunteer for additional screening in advance and thereby become eligible for expedited processing at POEs (see "Trusted Traveler Programs").

Pre-Travel Screening

Most foreign nationals seeking to enter the United States must get permission to do so prior to travel, and are subject to pre-travel screening. With the exception of U.S. LPRs,[31] certain Canadian citizens,[32] and certain residents of Caribbean islands other than Cuba,[33] foreign nationals seeking admission to the United States must apply in advance for a nonimmigrant visa[34] at a U.S. consulate abroad (see "Consular Reviews"), or in certain cases through an on-line process for permission to participate in the U.S. Visa Waiver Program (see "Visa Waiver Program"). Air passengers are subject to further screening at several points during the lead-up to their U.S.-bound flights (see "Air Passenger Screening").

Consular Reviews[35]

Before applying for admission at a U.S. port of entry, aliens seeking to visit the United States generally must obtain a visa at a U.S. consulate abroad. Visa applicants are required to submit biographic and biometric data, and usually must participate in an in-person interview. Applicants also may be subject to physical and mental examinations. Consular reviews are designed to ensure that aliens do not receive a visa to visit the United States if they are inadmissible for any of the reasons identified in INA §212, including health-related grounds, criminal history, security and terrorist concerns, indigence (likely to become a public charge), seeking to work without proper labor certification, ineligibility for citizenship, and certain previous immigration violations.

As part of the visa application process, DOS consular officers use the Consular Consolidated Database (CCD) to screen visa applicants. The CCD is a database of over 100 million visa and passport case records and 75 million photographs from 25 different DOS systems.[36] The CCD links automatically to the Consular Lookout and Support System (CLASS) database, which consular officers use to identify visa applicants on security watchlists or with other derogatory information, and to the Arrival and Departure Information System (ADIS) and the Automated Biometric Identification System (IDENT), which CBP officers use to screen arriving travelers at POEs (see "Text Box: Select Immigration Inspections Databases and Systems"). Consular officers refer high risk cases to DHS and other law enforcement agencies for Security Advisory Opinions (SAOs). If consular officers receive information about a foreign national that causes concern, they notify the National Counterterrorism Center (NCTC).

At certain consulates, the review process is further supplemented by the DHS Immigration and Customs Enforcement (ICE) Visa Security Program (VSP). Under this program, special agents at U.S. Immigration and Customs Enforcement (ICE) headquarters and in 20 high-risk consulates work with consular officers to examine visa applications for fraud, initiate investigations, coordinate with local law enforcement partners, and provide training and advice. The VSP Security Advisory Opinion Unit works with other law enforcement and intelligence agencies to provide a coordinated response when consular officers seek an SAO about a high risk case.[37]

Select Immigration Inspections Databases and Systems

Advance Passenger Information System (APIS): CBP database containing information about inbound air passengers and crew members. Air carriers submit passenger information to APIS prior to departing on U.S.-bound flights (or prior to arrival in the United States, in certain cases), and CBP uses the data to identify high-risk and inadmissible passengers.

Arrival and Departure Information System (ADIS): DHS database to collect and maintain biographic arrival and departure information on non-U.S. citizens traveling in and out of the United States. ADIS is maintained by CBP and the DHS Office of Biometric Identity Management (OBIM), and is the main database used by ICE to identify suspected visa overstayers.

Automated Biometric Identification System (IDENT): DHS's primary biometric database. Certain aliens' biometric records are added to IDENT upon admission to the United States, when aliens are apprehended or arrested by a DHS agency, and when aliens apply for certain immigration benefits.

Automated Targeting System (ATS): CBP database of incoming and certain outbound cargo and persons. Advanced screening information is added to the ATS and checked against intelligence data from CBP's National Targeting Center (NTC) and other intelligence and law enforcement databases to produce a risk-based score. Travelers above a certain ATS threshold generally are selected for secondary inspection.

Consular Lookout and Support System (CLASS): DOS database used by passport agencies, posts, and border inspection agencies to perform name checks on visa and passport applicants to identify subjects of terrorist lookouts and watchlists and other individuals who are ineligible for a visa or require other special action.

Electronic System for Travel Authorization (ESTA): Web-based CBP system that screens applicants to enter the United States through the Visa Waiver Program against terrorist, national security, and criminal watchlists.

Integrated Automated Fingerprint Identification System (IAFIS): Federal Bureau of Investigation (FBI) criminal database of fingerprints, criminal histories, photographs, and biographic information.

Biographic and biometric records may be checked against IAFIS to verify that aliens have not been convicted of crimes making them inadmissible to the United States.

Interagency Border Inspection System (IBIS): DHS database of shared law enforcement files related to individuals, businesses, vehicles, aircraft, and vessels with suspected criminal violations. IBIS is used by CBP officers at POEs, U.S. Citizens and Immigration Services (USCIS) officers making determinations about immigration benefits, and other U.S. and international law enforcement agencies involved with border enforcement.

National Crime Information Center (NCIC): FBI database for tracking federal, state, local, and tribal crime data. NCIC includes records of stolen vehicles and other articles, foreign fugitives, missing persons, gang members, known or suspected terrorists, and persons with outstanding criminal warrants, among other data.

National Targeting Center-Passenger (NTC-P): CBP, other DHS, and DOS officials at the NTC-P use the Automated Targeting System to screen passenger manifests and visa records against the Terrorist Screening Database and other national security records in order to prevent certain travelers from boarding U.S.-bound flights.

TECS (not an acronym): principal information-sharing system used by CBP officers at ports of entry to screen arriving travelers for admissibility to the United States. CBP officers use TECS to check travelers against law enforcement and national security watchlists and to record and report on primary and secondary inspection results.

Terrorist Identities Datamart Environment (TIDE): Classified database of known or suspected terrorists maintained by U.S. intelligence community. Data from TIDE are uses to populate the FBI's Terrorist Screening Database (TSDB).

Terrorist Screening Database (TSDB): Also known as the consolidated Terrorist Watchlist, the TSBD is maintained by the FBI's Terrorist Screening Center, and includes biometric and biographic records of known and suspected domestic and international terrorists.

Source: CRS analysis of Departments of Homeland Security, Justice, State, and Defense Privacy Impact Assessments and related documents.

Visa Waiver Program

The Visa Waiver Program (VWP) allows nationals from certain countries[38] to enter the United States as temporary visitors for business or pleasure (i.e., as B-1/B-2 nonimmigrants) *without* obtaining a visa from a U.S. consulate abroad. Thus, the program is designed to facilitate travel and tourism from low-risk countries, while also fostering positive relations with such countries, and holding down consular operating costs. In FY2012, about 19.1 million visitors entered the United States under the VWP program, constituting 40% of overseas visitors.[39]

Some Members of Congress have raised concerns that the VWP may weaken security because travelers are not required to provide biometric data when applying for admission through the program and are exempted from consular reviews. In addition, some people see the program as vulnerable to visa overstays since the entry-exit system has not been fully implemented (see "Entry-Exit System: Implementation").[40]

On the other hand, aliens seeking admission under the VWP are required to submit biographic information and respond to eligibility questions through an on-line Electronic System for Travel Authorization (ESTA). Upon receipt of an ESTA application, CBP screens applicants' data against TECS (not an acronym) and the Automated Targeting System (ATS; see "Text Box: Select Immigration Databases").[41] And aliens authorized for travel under the VWP must provide biometric data during primary inspection at a POE prior to entering the United States (see "Primary Inspections").[42] The program also likely enhances U.S. security because partner countries must meet specified document security and information-sharing requirements, and it benefits U.S. visitors to VWP countries because they receive reciprocal visa-free travel benefits.

Air Passenger Screening

CBP conducts additional pre-travel screening of all persons (including U.S. citizens) seeking to travel to the United States by air.[43] Upon a traveler's purchase of an airline ticket, commercial airlines are required to make Passenger Name Record (PNR) systems and data available to CBP up to 72 hours in advance of travel. When passengers check in for international flights to the United States, carriers are required to transmit passenger and crew manifests to CBP prior to securing aircraft doors before departure. Biographic traveler data (passport and travel itinerary information) is submitted to the Advance Passenger Information System (APIS).

Passenger PNR and APIS data (as well as visa and ESTA data) are forwarded to CBP's National Targeting Center (NTC), where they are vetted against intelligence and law enforcement databases, including the consolidated terrorist watchlist and Interpol's lost and stolen passport list. Data are matched against targeting rules through the ATS to identify risky travelers. The NTC may issue a no-board recommendation to air carriers, and/or flag travelers for a secondary inspection upon arrival at a U.S. POE (see "Secondary Inspections"). The NTC issued 3,181 no-board recommendations in FY2011; it issued 4,199 no-board recommendations in FY2012, and 5,378 no-board recommendations in FY2013.[44]

Under the Immigration Advisory Program (IAP) program, created in 2004, CBP officers also are posted at 11 international airports in 9 partner countries.[45] IAP officers review documents, conduct interviews, and identify high-risk travelers. They do not have enforcement authority, but may recommend that air carriers not board certain passengers for U.S.-bound flights, flag passengers for secondary inspection upon arrival, and notify host-state law enforcement agencies of suspected criminal violations. Building upon the IAP concept, CBP launched the Joint Security Program (JSP) in 2009. Currently operational in Mexico City and Panama City, the JSP performs similar functions as the IAP, but also addresses travelers on international flights *not* bound to or from the United States. The IAP and JSP issued 2,890 no-board recommendations in FY2011, 2,505 no-board recommendations in FY2012, and 3,501 no-board recommendations in FY2013.[46] As of November 22, 2013, The IAP and JSP had made a total of 19,998 no-board recommendations since the IAP's inception in 2004.[47]

Primary Inspections

CBP officers at ports of entry interview arriving travelers and check their travel documents to determine whether the person is admissible to the United States. Basic biographic information (e.g., name, travel document number, date and location of arrival) for all travelers (including U.S. citizens) is collected and stored within TECS (not an acronym), the principal information-sharing platform used by CBP officers for immigration screening and admissibility determinations.

Arriving travelers are subject to certain immigration, criminal, and national security background checks through the TECS system and the ATS, which identify certain travelers to be selected for secondary inspection (see

"Secondary Inspection"). In general, these primary inspection activities have become far more intensive during the post-9/11 period. For example, whereas CBP historically examined drivers' documents at land POEs but did not consistently examine passenger documents, since 2010 CBP has inspected documents for 100% of land travelers. And whereas only 5% of land travelers were subject to law enforcement database queries in FY2005, 97% of land travelers were subject to such queries in FY2013. Southern border inspection protocols have focused in particular on evolving threats related to drug trafficking organizations, smugglers, and unauthorized immigrants.[48]

Travelers are also validated against visa or visa waiver program records (for non-citizens) and against the APIS database (for all air travelers). Non-citizens arriving at air and sea ports are required to provide biometric data (fingerprints and digital photographs), which are added to the IDENT database and vetted against additional biometric databases (see "Text Box: Select Immigration Inspections Databases and Systems").

Travelers determined by the CBP officer to be admissible are allowed to enter the United States, though they may be subject to a separate customs and/or agricultural inspection. Travelers suspected for any reason of being inadmissible, including because of high ATS scores or derogatory information in the TECS system, are referred to secondary inspection for additional screening and/or a more thorough interview (see "Secondary Inspection").

Preclearance

Travelers from 15 airports in Canada, Ireland, the Bahamas, Bermuda, and Aruba may be eligible to be pre-cleared by CBP officers based abroad. Preclearance (sometimes referred to as preinspection) includes the same document inspection, interview, and (as necessary) secondary inspection as normally occurs at a U.S. port of entry, including customs and agricultural screening. Preclearance officers at partner airports are unarmed and do not have law enforcement authority, but officers may refer people suspected of host-state criminal violations to partner country law enforcement agencies. Travelers arriving in the United States following a preclearance inspection may depart the aircraft directly into the arriving airport as they would from a domestic flight.

CBP may initiate preclearance facilities at the request of a host government and pursuant to a formal agreement with such a government. Host governments are responsible for providing secure preclearance facilities, and CBP covers officer salaries (including certain overseas expenses).

CBP views passenger preclearance programs as enhancing U.S. security and reducing deportation costs because such programs screen passengers earlier in the travel process, preventing the arrival of inadmissible travelers, as well as illegal weapons, agricultural products, etc., on U.S. soil.[49] The programs also speed lawful travel by reducing congestion at U.S. airports, and they allow international travelers to take advantage of tighter U.S. connection times.

In April 2013, DHS reached an agreement with the government of the United Arab Emirates (UAE) to set up a preclearance facility in the Abu Dhabi International Airport.

Some Members of Congress have raised objections to the proposed Abu Dhabi program because no U.S. air carriers fly directly from Abu Dhabi to the United States, arguably giving the UAE-owned Etihad Airlines a competitive advantage over U.S.-owned carriers, and because UAE is not a signatory to the United Nations Refugee Convention.[50] House appropriators included language in the House's FY2014 DHS Appropriations report to limit funding for preclearance operations in new locations unless an economic impact analysis of the new location on U.S. air carriers has been conducted and provided to the committee, among other conditions.[51]

I-94 Arrival/Departure Records

Certain classes of nonimmigrants visiting the United States for a temporary period are issued an I-94 arrival/departure record upon admission.[52] The I-94 record indicates the date of admission, class of admission (i.e., visa category), and visa expiration date. For travelers arriving at land ports, the I-94 consists of a paper form stapled to the foreign passport. Travelers are supposed to surrender the I-94 upon departure; and CBP may use I-94 receipts to track nonimmigrant exits and identify visa overstays. In practice, however, this system has proven difficult to implement, and paper I-94 receipts often are not collected from departing travelers.

In 2013, CBP discontinued issuing paper I-94 forms for travelers arriving at air and sea ports. CBP now uses the APIS system and information collected by the State Department and by CBP officers at ports of entry to create electronic arrival/departure records for these travelers.[53] In place of paper I-94 receipts for exiting air and sea travelers, CBP relies on carrier exit manifests (passenger lists) to confirm passenger departures (see "Entry-Exit System: Implementation").

Secondary Inspections and Immigration Enforcement

Travelers who trigger an alarm in the ATS, who are the subject of certain derogatory information in TECS, or who arouse suspicion (through their behavior, responses to questions, or suspicious documents) during primary inspection may be referred for secondary inspection. A small sample of travelers at certain POEs also is randomly selected for secondary inspection (see "Random Compliance Examination (COMPEX) Program"). Travelers at land POEs who are required to obtain I-94 arrival/departure records (see "I-94 Arrival/Departure Records") also are automatically referred to secondary inspection, where I-94s are issued. In general, travelers selected for secondary inspection may be subject to a more extensive interview and/or a physical search, as well as being subject to vetting against additional databases. At land POEs, travelers selected for secondary inspection (in contrast with other land travelers) must provide fingerprints data to be vetted against IDENT and other biometric databases (see "Text Box: Select Immigration Inspections Databases and Systems").

Inspection Outcomes

Table 1 describes primary and secondary inspections by mode of entry for FY2005-FY2012. As **Table 1** indicates, *primary inspections* at air and sea POEs fell slightly in FY2008 - FY2009, likely as a result of the global economic downturn, and inflows have increased since that time.

Overall, inspections at air POEs increased about 19% in FY2005-FY2013, from about 86 million to about 102 million. Inspections at land ports fell more sharply, dropping every year FY2005- FY2011, before recovering slightly in FY2012-FY2013. At 242 million, land inspections in FY2013 were down 31% from the FY2005 total of 318 million. As a result of these trends, the total number of inspections fell from 420 million in FY2005 to 340 million in FY2011, before climbing back to 362 million in FY2013; and the proportion of all primary inspections occurring at land POEs fell from about 75% in FY2005 to about 67% in FY2013.

As **Table 1** also indicates, an increasing share of travelers was subject to *secondary inspections* during FY2005-FY2013. This trend exists across all three modes of entry, but was most pronounced at air POEs, where the proportion of travelers subject to secondary inspection increased from 2.0% in FY2005 to 6.4% in FY2010, before falling to 5.2% in FY2013 (5.3 million out of 102 million).[54]

Table 1. CBP Primary and Secondary Inspections, by Mode of Entry, FY2005-FY2013

Fiscal Year	Air POEs			Sea POEs			Land POEs		
	Primary	Secondary	Admissions	Primary	Secondary	Admissions	Primary	Secondary	Admissions
2005	86,067,723	1,730,318	85,990,506	15,951,767	NA	15,949,121	317,765,243	37,948,279	317,593,950
2006	87,844,145	2,035,959	87,796,222	15,958,508	NA	15,954,701	309,040,051	38,642,595	308,884,218
2007	91,650,242	4,926,793	91,606,534	18,347,270	89,834	18,334,501	297,680,056	38,445,467	297,534,607
2008	94,682,417	5,134,373	94,640,917	17,713,383	124,628	17,660,532	289,085,271	29,224,646	288,956,502
2009	87,749,074	5,373,858	87,704,806	16,928,474	154,081	16,863,944	256,514,233	29,952,109	256,399,212
2010	91,488,268	5,826,930	91,444,665	17,898,302	240,505	17,830,156	243,594,037	33,707,702	243,477,680
2011	94,604,610	5,558,384	94,566,280	18,757,561	241,041	18,691,407	226,984,093	32,429,991	226,877,381
2012	98,341,220	5,619,071	98,326,666	19,430,410	162,144	18,282,937	234,897,863	33,612,004	234,797,985
2013	102,221,415	5,342,236	102,172,540	17,882,894	130,908	17,831,338	242,064,137	29,879,235	241,960,854

Source: Data provided by CBP Office of Field Operations, December 30, 2013.

Notes: Complete data for secondary inspections at seaports were not available for FY2005-FY2006. Airport secondary inspection data excludes pre-clearance airports (about 17% of air travelers) and private aircraft and crew (less than 1% of air travelers).

At sea POEs, the proportion of travelers subject to secondary inspection increased from 0.49% in FY2007 (the first year for which data are available) to a high of 1.3% in FY2010, to 0.7% in FY2013. And at land POEs, the proportion of travelers subject to secondary inspection increased from 11.9% in FY2005 to about 14% in FY2010-FY2012, before falling back to 12.3% in FY2013. At land ports, the increase in the secondary inspection rate has been a function of the *fall* in total travelers at such ports, not an increase in the number of secondary inspections.

A final observation about **Table 1** is that the great majority of travelers inspected at POEs are determined to be *eligible for admission*. Overall, the annual rate at which persons inspected at POEs were admitted to the United States remained steady at between 99.94% and 99.95% in FY2005-FY2013. (Put another way, about 5 out of 10,000 people arriving at a POE are denied admission.) Approval rates were similar across air, sea, and land modes of entry.

Immigration Enforcement

Pursuant to 8 C.F.R. 235.1, the burden of proof is on the traveler to demonstrate to a CBP officer at a POE that the traveler is a U.S. citizen or an admissible foreign national. In general, a person arriving at a POE who is determined to be ineligible for admission may be subject to similar sanctions as an unauthorized alien present in the United States, including four main outcomes:

- **Withdrawal of application**: Pursuant to INA §235(a)(4), a CBP officer may permit an alien applying for admission to withdraw his or her application for admission and depart immediately from the United States. An alien withdrawing an application is not subject to additional penalties (i.e., a withdrawal does not result in a period of inadmissibility), but a record of the withdrawal is added to the alien's file and may influence a future visa eligibility determination.

- **Standard removal**: In general, an alien at a POE whom CBP determines to be inadmissible under INA §212 may be subject to removal from the United States under INA §240. Pursuant to INA §239, a CBP officer may initiate removal proceedings by serving an alien with written notice, known as a notice to appear (NTA). Pursuant to §240, an alien facing such removal proceedings generally may appear before an immigration judge and may be eligible to seek certain types of discretionary relief from removal. An alien who is formally removed from the United States generally is ineligible for a visa (i.e., is inadmissible) for at least five years,[55] and may be subject to criminal charges if he or she illegally reenters the United States.[56]

- **Expedited removal**: Pursuant to INA §235(b), an alien arriving at a POE without documents or with fraudulent documents and who does not indicate a fear of persecution may be subject to "expedited removal" (ER). Under this provision, an alien may be formally removed by order of a CBP officer without appearing before an immigration judge and without being eligible for certain forms of relief. Aliens removed by ER are subject to the same penalties as aliens removed under INA §240.

- **Criminal arrest**: CBP may arrest individuals (including U.S. citizens) at land, sea, and air POEs on the basis of an outstanding federal, state, local, or tribal criminal warrant; in response to a suspected violation of federal immigration-related crimes; or in response to a suspected violation of other federal border-related crimes, including smuggling crimes.

Table 2 describes selected immigration enforcement outcomes at ports of entry for FY2005- FY2012. As Table 2 indicates, there is no clear, sustained trend in three categories of interest: the overall number of aliens denied admission during this period has fluctuated between about 253,000 aliens in FY2005 and about 195,000 aliens in FY2012; the number of aliens issued a notice to appear (i.e., placed in standard removal proceedings) has fluctuated between about 15,000 aliens in FY2005 and about 24,000 aliens in FY2007 and FY2013 (consistently between 6 and 12% of aliens denied admission);[57] and the number of persons arrested on criminal charges or warrants has fluctuated between about 23,000 and 28,000.

Table 2 also reveals two apparent trends in enforcement outcomes at POEs. First, the number of aliens permitted to withdraw their applications for admission has fallen steadily from about 96,000 in FY2005 to about 52,000 in FY2013. According to CBP, this reduction is explained, at least in part, by a 2008 OFO directive permitting officers to exercise discretion in certain cases where applicants for admission are technically inadmissible due to a minor documentary deficiency, such as a recently expired passport or nonimmigrant visa. In such cases, aliens may be permitted to correct their documentation and reapply for admission at a later date and time without being required to formally withdraw an application for admission.[58]

Table 2. Immigration Enforcement at Ports of Entry, Selected Outcomes FY2005-FY2013

Fiscal Year	Total Admitted	Total Denied Admission	Withdrawal of Application	Notice to Appear	Expedited Removal	Criminal Arrests
2005	419,533,577	253,041	96,081	15,371	55,546	23,214
2006	412,635,141	209,437	93,022	22,445	45,983	23,448
2007	407,475,642	203,313	97,649	23,779	41,379	24,357
2008	401,257,951	224,705	85,157	21,259	38,808	24,347
2009	360,967,962	225,073	72,729	17,896	37,914	28,273
2010	352,752,501	231,045	75,866	19,189	38,590	27,868
2011	340,135,068	215,248	62,726	17,667	40,531	25,989
2012	351,407,588	195,142	55,171	21,928	34,802	24,087
2013	361,964,732	204,633	52,104	23,730	34,826	24,187

Source: Data provided by CBP Office of Legislative Affairs, December 30, 2013.
Notes: In addition to the categories listed in this table, aliens denied admission include crewmembers detained on board vessels (i.e., denied shore leave), persons paroled into the United States, persons permitted to enter with deferred inspection orders, persons granted voluntary return, and visa waiver program travelers refused admission, among others. Criminal arrests include U.S. citizens.

Second, the number of aliens placed in expedited removal fell by about one-third between FY2005 and FY2009 (from about 55,000 to about 38,000), and has remained roughly flat since that time. It is not clear whether the initial drop in ER cases reflected a policy change, a change in the demographics of arriving aliens, or a statistical anomaly. Overall, the data in Table 2 do *not* appear to reflect a significant shift at POEs toward "high consequence" enforcement outcomes (i.e., an increase in the proportion of removable aliens facing criminal charges and/or formal removal). This trend stands in contrast to enforcement trends *between* ports of entry, where the Border Patrol has more systematically implemented CBP's Consequence Delivery System.[59]

Random Compliance Examination (COMPEX) Program

CBP's Random Compliance Examination (COMPEX) was established by the legacy U.S. Customs Service in 1999 to gather information about the effectiveness of the passenger inspections process, and CBP expanded the program after the creation of DHS to also encompass more general immigration and agricultural inspection activities. The program selects a random sample of vehicles and air passengers who would be cleared for admission to the United States during primary inspection, and subjects the sample to a detailed secondary examination. CBP counts violations detected in the sample of otherwise-cleared travelers to estimate the number of undetected violations.

In FY2012, CBP reports that the COMPEX program was operational at 19 commercial airports representing over 80% of traveler volume, and at 105 land POEs representing over 94% of private vehicle volume.[60] The program conducted over 640,000 random secondary inspections, including 184,000 air passengers and 456,000 vehicles at land POEs. Overall, a very small percentage of travelers in the sample were found to have committed a major violation.[61]

Theoretically, the COMPEX program offers a powerful tool to estimate illegal flows and CBP's effectiveness rate at POEs. Whereas developing accurate and reliable estimates of illegal flows and of the effectiveness of enforcement between POEs is notoriously difficult because of uncertainty about the number of unobserved inflows,[62] detailed secondary inspections on a sample of inflows at POEs should produce an accurate count of violations within this group. And as long as the sample is statistically valid, CBP could use COMPEX results to estimate total illegal inflows and the apprehension rate at POEs.

On the other hand, COMPEX is limited in some respects as a tool for describing illegal immigration flows. One limitation is that the program covers air passengers and personal vehicles at land POEs, but does not cover sea passengers, pedestrians at land POEs, or most cargo operations.[63] Second, while a CBP officer may order the collection of biometric data as part of a COMPEX secondary inspection, such data is not collected systematically. As a result, while the program likely detects certain types of illegal migration through POEs (i.e., unauthorized immigrants hidden within passenger vehicles), COMPEX is not designed to detect certain other illegal inflows (i.e., unauthorized immigrants hidden within cargo containers or unauthorized immigrants using fraudulent documents or documents belonging to another person—not to mention flows of legal visitors who eventually overstay a nonimmigrant visa).

A third limitation is that while COMPEX is designed to produce a statistically valid estimate of the overall number of POE violations, the program is *not* designed to measure violations within specific subcategories of flows, including the subcategory of illegal migration.[64] In addition, while sampling at land POEs is based on the random assignment of cases through the TECS system, sampling at airports is based on the manual selection of cases by port managers and senior officers, which may introduce sample bias.

Reportedly, COMPEX inspections also may be suspended at certain ports and certain times in order to speed processing times.[65] For all of these reasons, it is not possible, based on COMPEX findings, to draw reliable inferences about total illegal inflows through POEs.

A final concern about COMPEX is that information about the program has not been widely available. CBP considers such information law-enforcement sensitive, and does not publish information about COMPEX results or methodology; Congress has never held a public hearing on the program; and it has never been the subject of an extensive Government Accountability Office (GAO) study.[66] These limitations make it difficult to evaluate the program or to weigh potential program reforms (also see "Illegal Migration through Ports of Entry").

Trusted Traveler Programs

Pursuant to §7209(k) of the IRTPA, CBP manages a number of "trusted traveler" programs that permit travelers to voluntarily provide detailed biometric and biographic data to CBP, and thereby to be eligible for expedited admission at POEs. Trusted traveler programs are designed to facilitate the admission of known, low-risk travelers and to strengthen security by focusing enforcement resources on unknown travelers (also see "Trusted Traveler Programs: Issues for Congress").

Global Entry

The main trusted trader program is Global Entry, which is open to U.S. citizens and LPRs, Dutch citizens, South Korean citizens, and Mexican nationals. Canadian nationals also may receive Global Entry benefits by joining NEXUS (not an acronym; see "NEXUS").[67] In addition to meeting the nationality requirement, Global Entry applicants must *not*

- provide false or incomplete application information;
- have any previous criminal convictions or outstanding warrants;
- have any previous immigration violations;
- be the subject of an ongoing criminal investigation;
- be inadmissible to the United States;
- have any known or suspected terrorist connections; or
- be unable to satisfy CBP that they are low risk.

Applicants are required to provide biometric data and participate in an in-person interview. Applicants are checked against a variety of national security and criminal databases during the initial application and upon each visit to the United States; and the entire trusted traveler list also is subject to regular re-checks against certain databases.

In general, Global Entry members are eligible for expedited processing at participating POEs, which include 44 airports in the United States, Canada, Ireland, Guam, Northern Mariana Islands, and Puerto Rico.[68] Instead of the normal primary and customs inspections, members present their machine-readable travel documents (via a card-swipe system), fingerprints (via a scanner), and customs declarations (via touchscreen) at an automated Global Entry kiosk. In most cases, the kiosk issues a receipt, and travelers may claim their bags and exit into the airport without further inspection. Global Entry members still may be selected for secondary inspection on the basis of derogatory information during the screening process or at random.

NEXUS

NEXUS (not an acronym) is a jointly-managed U.S.-Canadian trusted traveler program. NEXUS applicants must meet similar eligibility requirements as those for Global Entry, and must be approved by both countries. As noted, NEXUS members automatically are eligible to use Global Entry kiosks and enjoy similar benefits at Global Entry locations. NEXUS members also receive a secure, Radio Frequency Identification (RFID)[69] photo ID card that is Western Hemisphere Travel Initiative (WHTI) compliant, and that offers expedited processing through dedicated NEXUS travel lanes at 20 land POEs on the U.S.-Canadian border.[70]

Secure Electronic Network for Travelers Rapid Inspection (SENTRI)

The Secure Electronic Network for Travelers Rapid Inspection (SENTRI) program is a trusted traveler program that provides similar benefits at the U.S.-Mexico border as NEXUS provides at the U.S.-Canada border. SENTRI members receive a WHTI-compliant RFID card, which may be used at 11 land POEs.[71] Unlike NEXUS, SENTRI is not jointly managed by the United States and Mexico. SENTRI members also must register their vehicles with the program, and may only use SENTRI lanes while driving registered vehicles. SENTRI applicants are subject to somewhat more stringent application requirements, and must provide

- original evidence of citizenship;
- original evidence of admissibility to the United States (for non-U.S. citizens);
- driver's license or state ID document;
- vehicle registration and proof of insurance or a notarized letter authorizing use of the vehicle if the SENTRI applicant is not the vehicle owner;
- evidence of employment or financial support; and
- evidence of residence.

Table 3 summarizes cumulative trusted traveler program membership for FY2009-FY2013. As Table 3 indicates, all three programs have grown substantially during this period, with NEXUS and SENTRI growing five-fold and seven-fold, respectively, and Global Entry growing by a factor of 45. As of FY2013, Global Entry and NEXUS each counted over 900,000 members, while SENTRI included almost 360,000.

Table 3. Cumulative Membership in CBP Trusted Traveler Programs, FY2009-FY2013

Fiscal Year	Global Entry	NEXUS	SENTRI
2009	20,166	141,537	44,242
2010	76,435	457,630	229,224
2011	200,380	589,871	263,937
2012	431,004	737,302	301,889
2013	935,510	900,499	357,731

Source: CBP Office of Congressional Affairs, December 30, 2013.
Note: Enrollment figures for each fiscal year are cumulative.

Table 4. Annual Travelers Admitted, CBP Trusted Traveler Programs, FY2010-FY2013

Fiscal Year	Global Entry	NEXUS	SENTRI
2010	344,161	2,843,861	12,520,286
2011	893,532	3,784,569	15,866,233
2012	1,670,790	5,114,107	17,816,896
2013	2,785,205	5,902,762	19,743,147

Source: CBP Office of Congressional Affairs, December 30, 2013.

Table 4 describes the annual number of travelers admitted through NEXUS and SENTRI lanes and Global Entry kiosks in FY2010-FY2013. As Table 4 indicates, trusted traveler flows have also increased during this period, though not as quickly as program membership, with Global Entry flows increasing seven-fold since FY2010, NEXUS flows doubling during this period, and SENTRI flows growing by about 50%.

OUTBOUND ENFORCEMENT

At certain land ports on the Southern border, travelers may be subject to screening and potential inspection as they depart the United States. Outbound enforcement is managed by the Outbound Programs Division within the Office of Field Operations. The division's mandate focuses on addressing violence in Mexico and the Mexico-United States drug trade by interdicting illegal currency, arms, and ammunition outflows. DHS reports that about 700 CBP officers participate in the outbound enforcement program.[72]

Table 5 describes annual seizures by the Outbound Programs Division for FY2009-FY2013. As Table 5 indicates, outbound enforcement seized a total of about 5,100 kilograms of illegal drugs during this period in 3,442 separate seizure incidents; $221 million worth of illegal currency exports; 8,210 illegal weapons, and about 12.1 million rounds of ammunition. Some experts view the number of southbound drug seizures—almost 3 per day in FY2013—as an indicator of the global nature of the market for illegal drugs, and of the United States' emerging role as a transshipment country for illegal drugs. At the same time, while seizure incidents have increased since FY2009, the average seizure size fell sharply in FY2013. Illegal currency and ammunition seizures are also down since FY2009 and FY2010, respectively. It is not clear whether the recent drop in illegal drug volume and the sustained drops in currency and ammunition seizures reflect changes in tactics by drug trafficking organizations or are statistical anomalies.

Some people have argued that the United States should place greater emphasis on outbound enforcement to disrupt transnational criminal operations. According to this view, preventing U.S.- Mexico money and currency flows would eliminate the incentive for Mexico-U.S. drug flows, while also reducing criminal organizations' firepower.[73]

Table 5. CBP Outbound Enforcement Seizures, FY2009-FY2013

Fiscal Year	Illegal Drugs (kilograms)	Illegal Drugs (incidents)	Currency (dollars)	Weapons	Ammunition Rounds
2009	336	438	58,120,418	435	2,237,619
2010	878	527	46,813,819	2,351	7,340,472
2011	1,434	549	47,303,379	1,986	1,960,636
2012	1,911	897	31,665,153	653	213,579
2013	540	1,031	37,122,471	2,785	387,724
Total	5,099	3,442	221,025,240	8,210	12,140,030

Source: CBP Office of Congressional Affairs December 30, 2013.

Outbound enforcement efforts confront a number of challenges, however. Laws restricting international currency transfers are notoriously difficult to enforce.[74] Outbound enforcement also takes resources away from inbound inspections, so that increasing outbound screening may add to inbound delays or compromise inbound security. In addition, most outbound lanes are not equipped with inspection infrastructure, leaving officers exposed to the elements and to nearby traffic flows.[75] Limited outbound lanes also mean that inspections may result in long waits for outbound travelers. Partly to address these concerns, outbound enforcement operations are normally short-term surges, followed by periods of reduced inspections.[76] Yet some analysts have argued that sophisticated criminal organizations can defeat enforcement surges by monitoring outbound lanes, and by suspending high value outflows whenever a surge is underway.

ENTRY-EXIT SYSTEM: IMPLEMENTATION

As noted elsewhere, section 110 IIRIRA, as amended, requires DHS to implement an automatic, biometric entry-exit system that covers all non-citizen travelers into and out of the United States and that identifies visa overstayers (see "Entry-Exit System: Legislative Requirements"). Prior to 1997, the INS collected entry-exit data manually by obtaining paper copies of traveler's I-94 records (see "I-94 Arrival/Departure Records"), and an INS contractor manually keyed in data from the forms. This system was unreliable because paper forms were not consistently collected (particularly departure forms); forms were not timely provided to the contractor; and data input errors were widespread.[77] INS initiated a pilot program in 1997 to further automate I-94 data collection by having airlines provide magnetic stripe I-94 arrival cards.

Passengers passed the cards to INS agents at POEs during primary inspection. The automated system also proved problematic, however, because airlines were reluctant to participate, because departure cards still were not reliably collected, and because the system did not cover land travelers, among other shortcomings.[78]

With the passage of new entry-exit mandates in 2000-2001 (see "Entry-Exit system: Legislative Requirements") and the creation of the Department of Homeland Security (DHS) in 2002, the U.S. Visitor and Immigrant Status Indicator Technology (US-VISIT) program was established within DHS in 2004 to manage the entry-exit system. US-VISIT was renamed the Office of Biometric Identity Management (OBIM) in March 2013.[79] CBP works with OBIM to collect and manage entry-exit data as described below.

Entry-Exit Databases

Entry-exit data are stored in two DHS databases: the Arrival and Departure Information System (ADIS) and the Automated Biometric Identification System (IDENT).

Arrival and Departure Information System (ADIS)

ADIS includes biographic traveler identification data (name, date of birth, nationality, gender, passport number and country, U.S. visa number, and related information), arrival and departure information (POE and travel date), and a person-specific Fingerprint Identification Number System (FINS) identifier that allows ADIS to be cross-referenced with the IDENT system (see "Automated Biometric Identification System (IDENT)").[80] Although ADIS includes the FINS biometric identifier, ADIS is a *biographic* database because its records are populated by reading identity documents, rather than by capturing fingerprints or other physiological data directly from the traveler. As of September 30, 2013, ADIS included over 280 million unique records.[81]

Automated Biometric Identification System (IDENT)

IDENT includes biographic data (including name, aliases, date of birth, phone numbers, addresses, nationality, personal descriptive data), biometric identifiers (including fingerprints and photographs), and information about subjects' previous immigration enforcement histories (including previous immigration apprehensions and arrests). IDENT is a fully *biometric* database that makes use of fingerprint scanners and digital cameras to collect physical data directly from database subjects. As of September 30, 2013, IDENT included over 160 million unique records.[82]

The IDENT database initially was designed to capture only index fingerprints (i.e., two prints per person), and mainly was conceived of as a tool for tracking foreign visitors and identifying visa overstayers. With the creation of the Federal Bureau of Investigation's (FBI's) Integrated Automated Fingerprint Identification System (IAFIS) in 1999,[83] the legacy Immigration and Naturalization Service (INS) and the FBI decided to integrate the IDENT and IAFIS databases to better identify criminal aliens. This integration eventually required the reconfiguration of IDENT as a ten-print system. It took several years to complete this transition, but by 2010 all CBP and Border Patrol locations had deployed fully integrated IDENT/IAFIS workstations.[84]

Particularly after the 9/11 attacks, the entry-exit system increasingly was seen as a national security tool for vetting arriving passengers. The USA PATRIOT Act required that the system be designed to permit background checks against relevant databases and identity verification throughout the visa application and admissions processes (see "Entry-Exit System: Legislative Requirements"). As of September 30, 2013, the IDENT security watchlist included 7.2 million people.[85]

Collection of Entry Data

Under US-VISIT/OBIM, the automated I-94 pilot program was discontinued, and entry data collection has been integrated into the immigration inspections process. In general, CBP officers collect entry data at ports of entry, and entry records automatically are added to the ADIS and (as appropriate) IDENT databases.

Entry data collection has been enhanced in three main ways in the post-9/11 period. First, pursuant to the Visa Waiver Permanent Program Act (P.L. 106-396) and the IRTPA (P.L. 108- 458), almost all travelers to the United States must present machine-readable passports or similarly secure travel documents to enter the country (see "Inspections for Admissions"). These standards are designed to improve *biographic* data collection by combatting document and identity fraud and reducing data input errors by automating information capture.

Second, beginning in 2004, US-VISIT deployed integrated biometric workstations (i.e., fingerprint scanners) at POEs to facilitate *biometric* data collection. Workstations were deployed at 115 airports and 14 sea ports beginning in January 2004, expanded to the 50 busiest land POEs by the end of 2004, and have been operational at almost all POEs since December 2006.[86]

Third, under a final rule published in 2009, all non-U.S. citizens entering the United States are required to provide biometric data with the exceptions of Canadian nationals admitted as visitors, LPRs returning from cruises that begin and end in the United States or entering at land ports of entry, Mexican nationals with border crossing cards (BCCs),[87] and travelers with other visas explicitly exempted from the program.[88] In practice, the 2009 rule means that virtually all arriving non-citizens at air and seaports (other than U.S. LPRs returning from U.S.-based cruises) are required to provide biometric data during primary inspection. At land ports, arriving passengers only provide biometric data in secondary inspection (see "Secondary Inspections"). It bears emphasis that while a relatively small number of visa *categories* are exempted from the biometric requirement, these exemptions cover the *majority of foreign visitors* to the United States.[89]

Collection of Exit Data

In general, the United States does not have a history of collecting exit data from departing travelers. (In contrast, European Union member states, among other countries, for many years have required that people pass through passport control booths not only upon admission to the country, but also prior to their departure.) As a result, DHS and its predecessor agency have confronted inadequate port infrastructure and staffing to readily implement exit data collection as required by existing law.

Since 2004, DHS has tested six exit data pilot programs and demonstration projects described below. Four of the programs have been described as problematic, and have been discontinued; but two programs involving biographic information sharing with air carriers and with the government of Canada have been described by DHS as successful, and are ongoing.

2004-2007: Air/Sea Exit Pilot Program

Between January 2004 and May 2007, US-VISIT tested three different biometric exit technologies at 12 airports and 2 seaports under the so-called Increment 1B Pilot Program. At different airports and seaports, the program tested biometric collection kiosks located inside secure checkpoints, biometric collection mobile devices located in departure gate areas, and a combination of kiosks and mobile validator devices. DHS's evaluation of the program reportedly found that all three technologies and scenarios successfully captured biometric and biographic information, and that data collection required between 60 and 90 seconds per passenger.[90]

Based on a series of reports in 2005-2007, GAO concluded in 2007 that the Increment 1B air and sea pilot had "not been managed well"; and GAO recommended that DHS discontinue the program. In addition to concerns about program planning, oversight, and analysis of alternatives, GAO found that only 24% of travelers subject to US-VISIT requirements complied with the exit procedures, and that the program lacked enforcement measures and had not evaluated the effect of adding such measures.[91] According to DHS's evaluation of the program, traveler compliance could be improved by integrating biometric data collection into the normal departure flow.[92]

2005-2006: Land Exit Proof of Concept

The lack of exit infrastructure and the potential for congestion as a result of exit data collection are viewed as particularly problematic at land POEs. Between August 2005 and November 2006, DHS operated a land exit proof-of-concept demonstration project at five ports of entry on the southern and northern borders to test the use of Radio Frequency Identification (RFID) technology for tracking departures. Under the project, RFID tags were added to about 200,000 I94 forms issued to nonimmigrant visitors.[93] The goal of the project was to capture exit data with minimal new infrastructure or DHS staffing and without adding to border congestion.[94]

RFID technology is limited to biographic data, however. In addition, based on the demonstration project, RFID data collection proved unreliable, with successful data collection from RFID tags rates as low as 14% at some ports, and with scanners unable to consistently distinguish between RFID entries and exits.[95] Thus, the conclusion drawn by GAO from the demonstration project was that RFID appears to be an inappropriate technology for exit data collection.[96]

2009: Air Exit Pilot Program

Between May and July of 2009, US-VISIT worked with CBP and the Transportation Security Administration (TSA) to operate a pair of biometric air exit pilot programs. At the Detroit airport, CBP officers collected biometric data from aliens subject to US-VISIT at departure gates for selected international flights. Data was usually collected in aircraft jetways, between air carrier boarding pass collection and travelers' entry onto aircraft. Certain CBP officers were assigned to review travelers' documents to identify people subject to the program, who were then referred to additional officers for data collection. At the Atlanta airport, TSA officers screened travelers prior to their entry into the TSA security checkpoint to identify people subject to US-VISIT requirements. Such people were referred to a special line within the checkpoint, where other TSA officers collected their biometric data.[97]

DHS concluded that the pilot generally confirmed that biometric data may be collected from departing travelers. During the course of the program, about 500,000 travelers were screened by CBP and TSA officers; about 30,000 were identified as subject to US-VISIT; and only one traveler refused to provide his biometric data.[98] Data collection only required a few seconds per passenger, and produced data of adequate quality for enrollment in IDENT.[99]

On the other hand, DHS also found that identifying travelers subject to US-VISIT requirements necessitated "extensive interaction" between screeners and travelers, that scaling up a program to cover all departures would greatly exceed available staffing capacity, that flight delays and related problems interfered with data collection, and that pilots and crew often boarded flights too early to be enrolled by CBP officers.[100] Locating US-VISIT screening and data collection at TSA checkpoints also had an impact on a large number of U.S. citizens and passengers scheduled for domestic flights;[101] and screening at TSA checkpoints arguably is less reliable than jetway screening when it comes to ensuring that people providing exit data actually leave the country.

In addition to these specific concerns, DHS's more extensive review of its biometric exit testing concluded that a comprehensive biometric air exit system "faces enormous cost and logistical challenges," with funding requirements projected to total about $3 billion over a 10 year period. For these reasons, in 2010 DHS adopted a plan to focus in the near-term on enhanced *biographic* data collection and analysis to identify potential overstayers, and to invest in research and development of emerging *biometric* technology to be employed in a *future* exit system.[102]

2009-2010: H-2A and H-2B Land Exit Pilot Program

In December 2009, US-VISIT and CBP initiated a pilot program to collect biometric data from exiting H-2A and H-2B temporary workers.[103] The pilot deployed kiosks adapted for outdoor use, and applied to certain H-2A and H-2B workers who entered and exited through the San Luis, AZ and Douglas, AZ POEs.[104] DHS reportedly plans to use information from the land exit pilot program to inform future land exit program planning,[105] but CRS has not been able to locate additional information about the program.

2008—Ongoing: Air Carrier Information Sharing

Since 2008, under the Advanced Passenger Information System (APIS) program, air and sea carriers are required to provide CBP with electronic copies of passenger and crew manifests prior to the departure of all international flights and voyages to or from the United States. For air carriers, such data must be provided prior to securing aircraft doors. CBP vets inbound passenger manifests against terrorist watchlist data, and CBP adds passenger arrival and departure data to the ADIS biographic database. According to DHS officials, air carrier compliance with APIS requirements has been close to 100% since 2010, and analysis of ADIS records allows DHS to identify air travelers who may have overstayed their visas (also see "Overstay Analysis").[106]

While DHS apparently views the APIS program as a viable system for tracking air and sea exits, the system may be seen as not meeting the entry-exit system's legislative requirements in at least three ways. First, although air and sea carriers review passengers' passports prior to issuing a boarding pass, APIS does not include a mechanism to authenticate biometric data (i.e., APIS only collects biographic data). Second, relatedly, the APIS system is not designed to reliably insure that the same individual who checks in for a flight or voyage actually boards the aircraft or vessel. Third, although APIS provides CBP with electronic passenger manifest lists, the manifests are generated by carrier agents during the check-in process; such "manual" data may be less secure than data collected directly from travelers' passports (i.e., "machine-readable" data).[107]

2012—Ongoing: U.S.-Canada Information Sharing

On February 4, 2011, President Obama and Canadian Prime Minister Harper signed a joint declaration describing their shared visions for a common approach to perimeter security and economic competitiveness: the Beyond the Border agreement.[108] Among other provisions, the agreement calls for the two countries to develop an integrated entry-exit system so that the record of a land entry into one country establishes an exit record from the other. The first phase of the program ran from September 2012 – January 2013, and included the exchange of biographic records for third country nationals and permanent residents (i.e., for persons other than U.S. or Canadian citizens) at four designated POEs. Canada was able to reconcile 94.5% of U.S. entries (i.e.,

Canadian exits) with Canadian immigration databases, and the United States was able to reconcile 97.4% of Canadian entries.[109] Based on these results, the countries initiated phase 2 of the pilot program in June 2013, expanding data collection to all automated POEs on the U.S.- Canada border. During phase 3, scheduled to begin in June 2014, biographic information also will be exchanged for U.S. and Canadian citizens traveling between the two countries.[110]

DHS apparently views the U.S.-Canadian integrated entry-exit system as a promising approach for collecting exit data at the northern border.[111] Under the current agreement, such information sharing will be limited to biographic data. DHS' ability to treat Canadian entry data as a reliable record of U.S. exits depends on both the organizational capacity of the Canada Border Services Agency (CBSA), and on a high level of trust and collaboration between CBSA and CBP.

Overstay Analysis

Within DHS, U.S. Immigration and Customs Enforcement's (ICE's) Overstay Analysis Unit identifies potential visa overstayers by matching ADIS arrival and departure records. ICE's Counterterrorism and Criminal Exploitation Unit (CTCEU) prioritizes certain overstay leads for further investigation. According to GAO's analysis of DHS data, DHS's enhanced biographic exit program reviewed a backlog of 1.6 million potential overstay records in 2011. About half of these cases (863,000) were found to have departed the United States or to have adjusted status. Out of the remaining records, along with 82,000 additional cases identified by CTCEU (i.e., a total of 839,000 records), DHS prioritized 1,901 (0.2% of overstayers; 0.1% of all cases initially reviewed) as possible national security or public safety risks. Further investigation of these high priority cases found that 1,013 individuals had departed the United States or adjusted to a lawful migration status, 9 individuals were arrested, and 481 individuals were the subject of ongoing ICE enforcement efforts as of March 2013, among other outcomes.[112]

The GAO also determined that about 1.2 million ADIS arrival records could not be matched to departure data, and raised questions about the quality of DHS's overstay data.[113] Moreover, DHS and its predecessor agency have not provided Congress with statutorily required reports on visa overstays since 1994, though then-DHS Secretary Janet Napolitano testified in February 2013 that the department would report to Congress by the end of the year.[114]

ISSUES FOR CONGRESS

Entry-Exit System: Issues for Congress

The completion of a more comprehensive entry-exit system has been a persistent subject of congressional concern. As discussed elsewhere, two limitations of the current system are that most people entering the United States by land POEs only provide biographic data (i.e., do not provide biometric data), and that DHS may not have a fully reliable system for overstay analysis (see "Entry-Exit System: Implementation"). DHS reportedly has made progress with respect to real-time overstay analysis, but did not publish estimated overstay rates that had been expected in 2013.[115] In addition, even when DHS identifies potential visa overstayers in its dataset, the department has limited ability to track down and remove such overstayers.[116]

Arguably, the biggest questions about the entry-exit system concern the collection of exit data. No exit data are collected from persons leaving through southern border land ports; and data collection at other ports is limited to biographic data, is not always based on machine-readable data, and relies on information sharing with Canada and with air and sea carriers. DHS reportedly believes that the biographic information sharing generally meets its needs for purposes of exit tracking at an acceptable cost,[117] and CBP has indicated, for purposes of immigration screening, that "[w]hile biometric information is growing in importance, the vast majority of data available for use at the POEs is biographical."[118] At the same time, DHS has also argued that strengthening biographic data collection is a necessary precursor to biometric data collection, and views a biographic system as a desirable long-term goal for the entry-exit system.[119] Members of Congress concerned with exit tracking may focus on the following questions:

- Are *biographic* data adequate for entry-exit tracking, or should *biometric* exit data collection be viewed as a priority?
- If biographic data are adequate, would an upgrade to *machine-readable* biographic data represent an improvement over the status quo?
- Is *information-sharing* using data provided by airlines and by Canada an acceptable model for exit data, of should DHS collect exit data directly?

- If information-sharing is acceptable, can a similar model be implemented on the *U.S.-Mexico border*, or does the Southern border require a different approach?
- If information-sharing is not acceptable, what *additional infrastructure and personnel* are required (and at what cost) for CBP to collect universal exit data?

Several bills in the 113th Congress include provisions related to exit data collection. The Border Security, Economic Opportunity, and Immigration Modernization Act (S. 744), for example, would require carriers to collect electronic machine-readable biographic data from departing air passengers, and would make the implementation of this system one of the "triggers" for the complete implementation of the bill's legalization provisions for certain unauthorized immigrants. The bill would require DHS, within two years of enactment, to establish a *biometric* exit system at the ten U.S. airports with the greatest volume of international air travel.[120] S. 744 also would require DHS to place 90% of aliens identified as visa overstays in removal proceedings or to otherwise resolve their cases, though the bill would not direct new funding or programs to follow-up such cases.[121] The Border Security Results Act of 2013 (H.R. 1417), as reported by the House Homeland Security Committee, would require DHS, within 180 days, to submit a plan to Congress either to immediately complete a biometric entry-exit system, or to implement an alternative program within two years.[122] And the Strengthen and Fortify Enforcement Act (H.R. 2278), as ordered reported by the House Judiciary Committee, would require the complete implementation of the biometric entry-exit system at all POEs within two years.

Illegal Migration through Ports of Entry

Discussions of immigration control and border security often focus on unauthorized flows between ports of entry; but unauthorized immigrants also enter through ports of entry, either illegally or by overstaying a nonimmigrant visa. Visa overstayers enter legally on temporary (nonimmigrant) visas but fail to depart before the visa expires. Unauthorized immigrants enter through ports of entry by using fraudulent documents (including counterfeit or altered documents, and legitimate documents that do not belong to them) or by evading inspection, for example by being hidden inside a vehicle.

A potentially important question for Congress, particularly in light of the ongoing debate about immigration reform, is *how much unauthorized immigration occurs through POEs?* A 2006 study estimated that 40-50% of unauthorized immigrants in the country at the time were visa overstayers, and this study remains the most recent reliable public estimate.[123] In addition, interviews conducted with current and former unauthorized migrants in 2009 found that one out of four illegal entrants from Mexico had entered illegally through a port, either hidden in a vehicle or using borrowed or fraudulent documents, and that aliens attempting illegal entry through a POE were half as likely to be apprehended as those crossing between the ports.[124]

DHS has not published an estimate of the total number of visa overstayers in the United States or of the rate of illegal immigration through POEs, though the department reportedly plans to report on visa overstayers, as noted elsewhere.[125] The department reportedly does *not* have plans to produce an estimate of illegal flows through POEs, and the COMPEX program is not currently designed to produce such an estimate (see "Random Compliance Examination (COMPEX) Program"). The program likely could be modified— primarily by increasing sample size—to produce such an estimate if Congress viewed such modifications as a priority, though CBP reportedly does not support such a change.[126]

Recent border security bills and appropriations have targeted a greater share of resources to enforcement between ports of entry than to inspections and enforcement at POEs (see "Port of Entry Infrastructure and Personnel"). Some legislation in the 113th Congress continues to focus on enforcement between the ports. For example, S. 744 would require DHS to develop a strategy to achieve "effective control" of Border Patrol sectors between ports of entry, but does not establish goals or metrics for enforcement at the ports. On the other hand, the Border Security Results Act of 2013 (H.R. 1417), as reported by the House Homeland Security Committee, would establish POE enforcement metrics, though it would not authorize new enforcement measures.

Port of Entry Infrastructure and Personnel

One potential strategy for speeding migration flows while also enhancing border security is to add POE personnel and infrastructure. For any given volume of incoming travelers, both the flow rate (or "service level") *and* the time spent on inspections are a positive function of the number of CBP officers on duty and the number of active travel lanes.[127] Conversely, according to a 2008 GAO report, infrastructure weaknesses increased the risk that vehicles could enter the United States without inspection; and staffing shortages contributed to morale problems, fatigue, lack of backup support, and safety issues, "increasing the potential that terrorists, inadmissible travelers, and illicit good could enter the country."[128] GAO revisited these concerns in 2011 and reported that that DHS was taking steps to address GAO's recommendations regarding staffing and infrastructure, but that CBP faced challenges in developing POE performance metrics.[129] CBP's Workload staffing model identifies a need for 3,811 additional CBP officers at POEs in FY2014,[130] and the Administration's FY2014 budget proposal included a request for 3,477 additional officers.[131]

To some extent, the Office of Field Operations (OFO) competes for resources with CBP's Border Patrol and with U.S. Immigration and Customs Enforcement (ICE).[132] The Border Patrol has grown about three times faster than OFO in the post-9/11 period.[133] Similarly, S. 744, would direct CBP to more than double the number of Border Patrol agents on the southwest border, while only authorizing a 16% increase in OFO officers.[134] Other bills in the 113th Congress would augment POE staffing, however.[135]

Recent fiscal pressures have been a barrier to POE personnel increases. During the FY2014 budget process, the Administration proposed to hire 3,477 additional CBP officers (about half through increased appropriations and half through fee increases), but House appropriators recommended slower personnel growth, with half the proposed funding.[136] Congress also authorized a pilot program in 2012 permitting CBP to enter into public-private partnerships (PPPs) with certain localities and permitting the private sector to fund improvements in border facilities and port services, including by funding additional CBP officers and underwriting overtime hours.[137] The Obama Administration has proposed expanding the public-private partnership pilot program by permitting CBP to accept donations to expand port operations, but Congress may not support such an expansion, and also may curtail the existing program.[138]

Trusted Traveler Programs: Issues for Congress

As noted elsewhere, one of CBP's primary tools for risk management at POEs is the use of trusted traveler programs, including Global Entry, NEXUS, and SENTRI (see "Trusted Traveler Programs").[139] Trusted traveler programs are designed to facilitate legal flows by allowing low-risk, known travelers to be exempted from certain screening and inspections *and also* to enhance security by allowing CBP officers to focus greater attention on higher-risk flows. The benefits of trusted traveler programs should increase with scale because moving more travelers into expedited lanes speeds overall processing times, and fewer unknown travelers mitigates the "needle in the haystack" challenge of enforcement at POEs. Thus, legislation in the 113th Congress would promote membership in trusted trade programs.[140]

Congress and CBP confront certain obstacles to expanding trusted traveler programs, however. The main incentive CBP can offer trusted travelers is to reduce the likelihood of secondary inspections; but doing so may encourage *mala fide* actors to enroll in these programs to game the system. In addition, at land POEs, travelers only benefit from an expedited inspections process if they are also able to take advantage of dedicated NEXUS or SENTRI lanes (i.e., so that the entire queue is subject to expedited processing). But CBP has limited capacity to add and extend dedicated lanes because many ports are located in urban areas with limited space for expansion,[141] though the agency has addressed this problem, to some extent, by using "active lane management" systems that adjust lane assignments based on real-time demand.

APPENDIX. ENTRY-EXIT SYSTEM LEGISLATION

Congress has enacted the following legislation concerning an entry-exit system:

- Illegal Immigration Reform and Immigrant Responsibility Act of 1996 (IIRIRA, P.L. 104-208, Div. C). Section 110 required the Attorney General, within two years of enactment (i.e., by September 30, 1998), to develop an automated entry and exit control system that would collect records of alien arrivals and departures and allow the Attorney General through online searches to match such arrivals and departures and thereby identify nonimmigrant aliens who remain in the United States beyond the periods of their visas (i.e., visa overstayers). The bill also required the Attorney General to annually report to Congress on the number of visa overstayers and their countries of origin.
- P.L. 105-259 and P.L. 105-277. These appropriations acts amended §110 of IIRIRA to extend the deadline for implementing the entry-

exit system to October 15, 1998 for airports and seaports and to March 30, 2001 for land POEs.

- Immigration and Naturalization Service Data Management Improvement Act (P.L. 106-215). The act amended IIRIRA §110 to describe the entry-exit system in greater detail; clarified that the system's mandate did not impose new documentary requirements on travelers to the United States; and imposed new deadlines of December 2003 for implementation of the entry-exit system at all U.S. airports and seaports, December 2004 for implementation of the system as the 50 busiest land POEs, and December 2005 for making data from the system available to immigration officers at all POEs. The act also authorized the Attorney General to make entry-exit system data available to other law enforcement officials for law enforcement purposes.

- Visa Waiver Permanent Program Act (P.L. 106-396). Section 205 amended INA §217 to require the Attorney General (separate and apart from IIRIRA §110) to develop and implement a fully automated entry and exit control system to collect arrival and departure records for aliens traveling in and out of the United States under the Visa Waiver Program (also see "Visa Waiver Program").

- Uniting and Strengthening America by Providing Appropriate Tools Required to Intercept and Obstruct Terrorism Act of 2001 (USA PATRIOT Act, P.L. 107-56). Section 411 encouraged the Attorney General to implement the IIRIRA entry-exit system "with all deliberate speed." The act directed the Attorney General, in the development of the system, to focus on the utilization of biometric technology and tamper-resistant documents; and it required that the system interface with law enforcement databases to identify individuals who pose a threat to national security. In addition, section 403 required the Departments of Justice and State, working through the National Institute of Standards and Technology (NIST), to develop and certify a technology standard that can be used to verify the identity and check the backgrounds of persons applying for a U.S. visa or seeking admission at a POE.

- Enhanced Border Security and Visa Entry Reform Act of 2001 (EBSVERA, P.L. 107-173). Section 302 required the Attorney General and DOS to use the technology standard required to be developed under the PATRIOT Act at POEs and at consular posts abroad; to establish an arrival and departure database; and to make all alien admissibility security databases interoperable.

- Intelligence Reform and Terrorism Prevention Act of 2004 (IRTPA, P.L. 108- 458). Among other provisions, section 7208 reiterated Congress's finding that a biometric entry-exit system should be implemented as expeditiously as possible and required DHS to develop and report on a plan to accelerate the full implementation of such a system. The section also clarified that the entry-exit system shall include a requirement for the collection of biometric data for all categories of individuals required to provide such data, regardless of the POE. And it imposed a two year deadline for the development of a fully interoperable data system among relevant agencies within DOS, DHS, and DOJ.
- Implementing Recommendations of the 9/11 Commission Act of 2007 (9/11 Act, P.L. 110-53). Section 711 amended INA §217 (as previously amended by P.L. 106-396) to require DHS within one year to establish an exit system to record the departure of all air travelers participating in the Visa Waiver Program.

End Notes

[1] Congressional Research Service (CRS) calculations based on data provided by U.S. Customs and Border Protection (CBP) Office of Legislative Affairs, December 30, 2013.

[2] Most CBP officers are based in the United States; some conduct immigration and cargo inspections abroad through partnership agreements with other countries. See in this report "Preclearance"; also see CRS Report R43014, *U.S. Customs and Border Protection: Trade Facilitation, Enforcement, and Security*.

[3] The Visa Waiver Program (VWP) allows nationals from certain countries to enter the United States as temporary visitors for business or pleasure *without* obtaining a visa from a U.S. consulate abroad; see in this report "Visa Waiver Program."

[4] "Aliens" is synonymous with non-citizens, including legal permanent residents, temporary nonimmigrants, and unauthorized aliens. Inadmissible aliens are aliens who are not permitted to enter the United States. Aliens may also be referred to as "foreign nationals."

[5] Section 110 of the Illegal Immigration Reform and Immigrant Responsibility Act of 1996 (IIRIRA, P.L. 104-208, Div. C) , as amended; see in this report "Entry-Exit System: Legislative Requirements."

[6] A similar tension exists with respect to cargo imports, which are beyond the scope of this report. See CRS Report R43014, *U.S. Customs and Border Protection: Trade Facilitation, Enforcement, and Security*.

[7] *Chae Chan Ping v. United States*, 130 U.S. 581, 9 S.Ct. 623. For a fuller discussion, see Thomas Alexander Aleinikoff, David A. Martin, and Hiroshi Mormura, et al., *Immigrtaion and Citizenship: Process and Policy* (St. Paul, MN: West Law, 2012), pp. 191-192.

[8] Aliens Act of July 6, 1798 (1 Stat. 566).

[9] Act of March 3, 1875 (18 Stat. 477). Provisions to exclude certain criminals, including aliens convicted of "crimes of moral turpitude" remain on the books under INA §212(a)(2). See CRS Report R41104, *Immigration Visa Issuances and Grounds for Exclusion: Policy and Trends.*

[10] The Chinese Exclusion Act of 1882 (22 Stat. 58) suspended immigration of Chinese laborers to the United States for 10 years; subsequent legislation made the ban permanent and eventually expanded it to the entire "Asia-Pacific triangle" (Immigration Act of 1917; 39 Stat. 874). The Quota Law of 1921 (42 Stat. 5) and the Immigration Act of 1924 (43 Stat. 153) established the "national origins quota system," which eventually set annual immigration quotas for the Eastern Hemisphere to match the ethnic demographics of the U.S. census of 1920.

[11] Immigration Act of March 3, 1903 (32 Stat. 1213).

[12] Internal Security Act of 1950 (64 Stat. 464).

[13] Immigration and Nationality Act (INA) of 1952 (P.L. 82-414; 66 Stat. 163).

[14] For a fuller discussion of threats at U.S. borders see CRS Report R42969, *Border Security: Understanding Threats at U.S. Borders.*

[15] CRS Report RL33874, *Unauthorized Aliens Residing in the United States: Estimates Since 1986,* by Ruth Ellen Wasem, *Population Decline of Unauthorized Immigrants Stalls, May Have Reversed,* Pew Research Center, Washington, DC, September 23, 2013.

[16] CRS Report RS22446, *Nonimmigrant Overstays: Brief Synthesis of the Issue.*

[17] Most cocaine, heroin, and methamphetamines smuggled into the United States enter through ports of entry in private, non-commercial vehicles (i.e., are admitted during immigration processing, rather than as cargo imports); most smuggled marijuana (along with certain other types of contraband) is hidden within legal commercial loads (i.e., enters through the customs process) or is smuggled between ports of entry. See U.S. Department of Justice, National Drug Intelligence Center, *National Drug Threat Assessment: 2011,* Washington, DC, 2011, p. 13.

[18] U.S. National Commission on Terrorist Attacks Upon the United States, *The 9/11 Commission Report: Final Report* (Washington: GPO, 2004). Hereafter: *9/11 Commission Report.*

[19] For a fuller discussion of threats at U.S. borders see CRS Report R42969, *Border Security: Understanding Threats at U.S. Borders.*

[20] World Bank, "International tourism, receipts," http://data.worldbank.org/indicator /ST.INT.RCPT.CD. This figure understates the full economic impact of international tourism since it does not account for certain non-travel and tourism goods purchased by international travelers.

[21] For a fuller discussion, see CRS Report R42969, *Border Security: Understanding Threats at U.S. Borders.*

[22] Pursuant to INA § 235A, added by the Illegal Immigration Reform and Immigrant Responsibility Act of 1996 (IIRIRA, P.L. 104-208, Div. C), preinspection stations are maintained at certain foreign airports, including airports identified as top points of departure for inadmissible aliens arriving at U.S. POEs. The United States implemented preinspection services at certain Canadian airports beginning in 1952; for a fuller discussion of preinspection services see, in this report, "Preclearance."

[23] Pursuant to 8 C.F.R. §235.1(b), a person claiming U.S. citizenship must establish that fact to the satisfaction of the inspecting officer, including by presenting a U.S. passport or other acceptable document; and a person who fails to meet these requirements is presumed for purposes of inspection for admission to be an alien.

[24] Sections 401-403 of the Homeland Security Act (P.L. 107-296) also transferred to the Department of Homeland Security (DHS) the duties of the U.S. Customs Service, and the Office of Field Operations (OFO) within CBP also is responsible for cargo inspections at ports of entry (POE). For a fuller discussion, see CRS Report R43014, *U.S. Customs and Border Protection: Trade Facilitation, Enforcement, and Security.*

[25] INA § 221, as amended; for a fuller discussion see CRS Report R41093, *Visa Security Policy: Roles of the Departments of State and Homeland Security.*

[26] Ibid.

[27] For a fuller discussion, see Department of Homeland Security, "Documents Required for Travelers Departing from or Arriving in the United States at Sea and Land Ports-of-Entry from within the Western Hemisphere," 73 *Federal Register* 18384, April 3, 2008.

[28] *9/11 Commission Report.*

[29] Acceptable documents include U.S. passport cards, enhanced driver's licenses, trusted traveler cards, U.S. military identification card, U.S. Merchant Mariner document, and enhanced tribal documents. See see CBP, "Document Requirements for Land and Sea Travel."

[30] Legal permanent residents (LPRs) are foreign nationals who come to live lawfully and permanently in the United States; see CRS Report R42866, *Permanent Legal Immigration to the United States: Policy Overview.*

[31] Pursuant to 8 C.F.R. §211, LPRs seeking admission to the United States generally must present a valid, unexpired immigrant visa, permanent resident card ("green card"), or other proof of identity and permanent resident status.

[32] Pursuant to 8 C.F.R. §212.1, Canadian citizens generally are not required to obtain a visa to enter the United States except under certain circumstances. Certain Canadian citizens also may apply to enter the United States as NAFTA Professionals (with TN nonimmigrant status) at a U.S. port of entry.

[33] Pursuant to 8 C.F.R. §212.1, citizens of the British overseas territory of Bermuda are not required to obtain a visa to enter the United States except under certain circumstances; residents of other Caribbean islands may be exempted from visa requirements under certain, more narrow conditions.

[34] Aliens seeking to come to the United States temporarily are known as nonimmigrants. These aliens are admitted to the United States for a temporary period of time and an expressed reason. For a fuller discussion, see CRS Report RL31381, *U.S. Immigration Policy on Temporary Admissions.*

[35] Except as otherwise noted, this section is based on CRS Report R41093, *Visa Security Policy: Roles of the Departments of State and Homeland Security*; see that report for a fuller discussion. Also see CRS Report R41104, *Immigration Visa Issuances and Grounds for Exclusion: Policy and Trends.*

[36] Department of State Privacy Coordinator, "Consular Consolidated Database (CCD) Privacy Impact Assessment (PIA)," March 22, 2010, http://www.state.gov/documents/organization /93772.pdf.

[37] Ibid. Also see Immigration and Customs Enforcement (ICE), *Congressional Budget Justification: FY2014*, pp. 36- 37.

[38] The list of participating countries as of September 2013 includes Andorra, Australia, Austria, Belgium, Brunei, Czech Republic, Denmark, Estonia, Finland, France, Germany, Greece, Hungary, Iceland, Ireland, Italy, Japan, Latvia, Liechtenstein, Lithuania, Luxembourg, Monaco, Malta, the Netherlands, New Zealand, Norway, Portugal, San Marino, Singapore, Slovakia, Slovenia, South Korea, Spain, Sweden, Switzerland, Taiwan, and the United

Kingdom. For a fuller discussion of the Visa Waiver Program, see CRS Report RL32221, *Visa Waiver Program*.

[39] DHS Office of Immigration Statistics, Yearbook of Immigration Statistics: FY2012, Table 25.

[40] See for example, U.S. Congress, House Committee on the Judiciary, Subcommittee on Immigration Policy and Enforcement, *Visa Waiver Program Oversight: Risks and Benefits of the Program*, 112th Cong., 1st sess., December 7, 2011.

[41] For a fuller discussion, also see DHS Privacy Office, "Privacy Impact Assessment for the Electronic System for Travel Authorization (ESTA)," June 2, 2008. In the first 11 months of FY2012, CBP vetted over 10.7 million ESTA applications, and denied more than 21,000 (0.2%) of them; see Testimony of CBP Assistant Commissioner Kevin McAleenan, U.S. Congress, House Committee on Homeland Security, Subcommittee on Border and Maritime Security, *Eleven Years Later: Preventing Terrorists from Coming to America*, 112th Cong., 2nd sess., September 11, 2012 (hereafter: McAleenan testimony, 2012).

[42] An alien found to be ineligible for VWP travel through ESTA still may apply for a visa before a U.S. consular officer.

[43] For a fuller discussion of CBP's air passenger screening procedures, see McAleenan testimony, 2012. Also see CBP, "Advance Electronic Transmission of Passenger and Crew Member Manfiests for Commercial Aircrafts and Vessels," 72 *Federal Register* 48320-48345, August 23, 2007.

[44] McAleenan testimony, 2012; CBP Office of Congressional Affairs, December 30, 2013. No-board recommendations are not binding, but carriers generally accept them to avoid the penalties and costs associated with transporting improperly-documented travelers.

[45] Participating airports include Amsterdam, Doha, Frankfurt, London Heathrow and Gatwick, Madrid, Manchester, Mexico City, Panama City, Tokyo and Paris.

[46] CBP Office of Congressional Affairs, December 30, 2013.

[47] Ibid.

[48] CBP Office of Congressional Affairs, December 30, 2013.

[49] CBP, "Fact Sheet: Preclearance Operations," May 2013.

[50] See for example, Letter from Hon. Michael McCaul, Hon. Bennie Thompson, Hon. Bill Shuster, et al. to Janet Napolitano, Secretary of Homeland Security, April 18, 2013; and U.S. Congress, House Committee on Foreign Affairs, Subcommittee on Terrorism, Nonproliferation, and Trade, *The Abu Dhabi Pre-Clearance Facility: Implications for U.S. Business and National Security*, 113th Cong., 1st sess., July 10, 2013.

[51] H.Rept. 113-91, p. 32.

[52] Nonimmigrants exempted from the I-94 requirement include Canadians admitted as visitors for business or pleasure and Mexicans with border crossing cards; see 8 C.F.R. §235.1(h).

[53] For a fuller discussion, see 78 *Federal Register* 18457.

[54] Data on secondary inspections at air POEs excludes preclearance airports (see in this report, "Preclearance"), which accounts for about 17% of air travel to the United States.

[55] INA §212(a)(9).

[56] INA §276.

[57] According to CBP (CRS communication with CBP Office of Congressional Affairs, December 30, 2013), the uptick in notices to appear observable since FY2011 reflects a pair of changes in recent years: in 2010 OFO directed a policy change to place certain arriving LPRs with criminal records in removal proceedings rather than permitting them to enter with deferred inspection orders, resulting in a rise in NTAs; and there has been an increase in the number of unaccompanied alien children arriving at ports of entry, who (pursuant to

the Trafficking Victims Protection Reauthorization Act of 2008) must be placed into removal proceedings and served with an NTA under certain conditions.

[58] CBP Office of Congressional Affairs, December 30, 2013.

[59] The Consequence Delivery System is a CBP program to promote formal removal, criminal charges, lateral repatriation, and other "high consequence" enforcement outcomes for aliens apprehended at the Southwest border; for a fuller discussion see CRS Report R42138, *Border Security: Immigration Enforcement Between Ports of Entry.*

[60] CBP Office of Congressional Affairs, March 31, 2013.

[61] Specific program results are considered law enforcement sensitive and are not available for publication.

[62] See CRS Report R42138, *Border Security: Immigration Enforcement Between Ports of Entry.*

[63] CBP is developing an expansion of COMPEX to extent to pedestrian crossing at land POEs; this component of the program is currently being pilot tested and is expected to become formally operational in FY2015.

[64] CBP Office of Congressional Affairs, December 30, 2013.

[65] See Testimony of National Treasury Employees Union President Colleen M. Kelley, U.S. Congress, House Committee on Homeland Security, Subcommittee on Border and Maritime Security, *Cargo Security Threats at Land Ports of Entry*, 111th Cong., 1st sess., October 22, 2009.

[66] The Government Accountability Office (GAO) initiated a major review of the COMPEX program in July 2001, but suspended the study following the 9/11 attacks; see GAO, *Customs and INS: Random Inspection Programs Can Be Strengthened*, GAO-02-215R, December 3, 2001. Other GAO work on COMPEX has been more limited.

[67] Eligibility criteria for Global Entry are defined in 8 C.F.R. §235.12.

[68] Pursuant to 8 C.F.R. §235.12, a list of participating Global Entry locations is available at http://www.globalentry.gov/locations.html.

[69] Radio Frequency Identification (RFID) is a contactless integrated circuit technology that permits scanners to read data tags quickly and remotely; EZ-Pass highway toll transponders are a familiar example.

[70] A list of ports with dedicated NEXUS lanes and hours of operation is available at http://cbsa-asfc.gc.ca/ prog/nexus/ land-terre-eng.html#where-ou.

[71] A list of ports with dedicated Secure Electronic Network for Travelers Rapid Inspection (SENTRI) lanes is available at http://www.cbp.gov/xp/cgov/travel/trusted_traveler /sentri/sentri.xml.

[72] See DHS, *U.S. Customs and Border Protection Salaries and Expenses*, Fiscal Year 2014 Congressional Budget Justification, p. 90.

[73] See CRS Report R41547, *Organized Crime: An Evolving Challenge for U.S. Law Enforcement*; also see Terry Goddard, *How to Fix a Broken Border: Hit the Cartels Where It Hurts*, American Immigration Council, Washington, DC, September 2011.

[74] Among other challenges, money may flow across the border in unrestricted amounts through "stored value" cards; and banks may permit questionable money transfers by establishing "funnel" accounts. See Ibid.; and GAO, *Challenges Exist in the Federal Government's Effort to Stem Cross-Border Currency Smuggling*, GAO-11-73, October 2010.

[75] See U.S. Government Accountability Office (GAO), *Moving Illegal Proceeds: Opportunities Exist for Strengthening the Federal Government's Efforts to Stem Cross-Border Currency Smuggling* GAO 11-407, March 9, 2011.

[76] See DHS, *U.S. Customs and Border Protection Salaries and Expenses*, Fiscal Year 2012 Congressional Submission, p. 90. In addition to these episodic surges, port officials have

told CRS that 100% of outbound vehicle and pedestrian traffic at some southwest border POEs is subject to visual screening (i.e., an officers watches outbound flows); and officers may temporarily close exit lanes to interview and/or inspect suspicious travelers.

[77] See Department of Justice, Office of Inspector General, *The Immigration and Naturalization Service's Automated I94 System,* 2001.

[78] Ibid.; also see GAO, *Information Technology: Homeland Security Needs to Improve Entry Exit System Expenditure Planning,* GAO-03-563, June 2003.

[79] The Office of Biometric Identity Management (OBIM) is a division within DHS's National Protection and Programs Directorate. The Administration's FY2014 budget request proposed (for the second year in a row) to eliminate USVISIT/OBIM and to transfer the entry-exit program into CBP and ICE, but both chambers rejected the Administration's proposed realignment during the FY2014 cycle. See CRS Report R43147, *Department of Homeland Security: FY2014 Appropriations.*

[80] For a fuller discussion of the Arrival and Departure Information System (ADIS), see 68 *Federal Register* 69412.

[81] Office of Biometric Identify Management (OBIM), Office of Congressional Affairs, November 15, 2013.

[82] Ibid.

[83] The Integrated Automated Fingerprint Identification System (IAFIS) database includes electronic ten-print records of more than 66 million subjects in its criminal master file along with more than 25 million civil fingerprints. See Federal Bureau of Investigation, "Integrated Automated Fingerprint Identification System," http://www.fbi.gov/about-us/cjis/ fingerprints_biometrics/iafis/iafis.

[84] For a fuller discussion of IDENT/IAFIS integration, see CRS Report RL32562, *Border Security: The Role of the U.S. Border Patrol.*

[85] Office of Biometric Identify Management (OBIM), Office of Congressional Affairs, November 15, 2013.

[86] According to a 2009 GAO report, US-VISIT was operational at all 115 airports, 14 seaports, and 154 of 170 land ports. US-VISIT was not deployed to the remaining land POE's because most visitors subject to US-VISIT requirements were not authorized to use them or because, in two cases, the ports did not have the necessary transmission lines to operate US-VISIT. See U.S. Government Accountability Office, *Homeland Security: Key US-VISIT Components at Varying Stages of Completion, but Integrated and Reliable Schedule Needed,* GAO-10-13, November 2009, p. 7, http://www.gao.gov/new.items/d1013.pdf.

[87] Border crossing cards (BCC, also known as "laser visas") are short-term multiple-entry, 10-year nonimmigrant visas that may be issued to certain citizens of Mexico for business or tourism. BCC holders are permitted to visit the United States for up to 30 days and must remain within a zone up to 25 miles from the border in Texas, New Mexico, and California or within 75 miles of the border in Arizona.

[88] U.S. Department of Homeland Security, Privacy Impact Assessment Update for the United States Visitor and Immigrant Status Indicator Technology Program (U.S.-VISIT) in Conjunction with the Final Rule (73 FR 7743), Enrollment of Additional Alien in US-VISIT," February 10, 2009.

[89] According to DHS data, there were about 165 million nonimmigrant admissions to the United States in FY2012, including about 54 million (33%) I-94 admissions (generally required to provide biometric data) and about 106 million tourists and business travelers from Canada and Mexicans with BCCs (generally exempted from the biometric requirement); see Randall Monger, *Nonimmigrant Admissions to the United States: 2012,* U.S. Department of

Homeland Security Office of Immigration Statistics, Annual Flow Report, August 2103, http://www.dhs.gov/sites/ default/files/publications/ois_ni_fr_2012.pdf.

[90] DHS, *US-VISIT Air Exit Pilots Evaluation Report, Fiscal Year 2009 Report to Congress*, Washington, DC, October 26, 2009, p. 60.

[91] GAO, *Homeland Security: Prospects for Biometric US-VISIT Exit Capability Remain Unclear*, GAO-07-1044T, June 28, 2007, pp. 7-8.

[92] DHS, *US-VISIT Air Exit Pilots Fiscal Year 2009 Report*, p. 60.

[93] Marc Songini, "DHS Nixes Use of RFID In Border Security Program," *Computer World*, February 15, 2007.

[94] For a fuller discussion, see GAO, *Border Security: US-VISIT Program Faces Strategic, Operational, and Technological Challenges at Land Ports of Entry*, GAO-07-378T, January 31, 2007.

[95] Ibid., pp. 18-19.

[96] GAO, *Homeland Security: Key US-VISIT Components at Varying Stages of Completion, but Integrated and Reliable Schedule Needed*, GAO-10-13, January 2009, p. 9.

[97] DHS, *US-VISIT Air Exit Pilots Fiscal Year 2009 Report*, pp. 5-8.

[98] Ibid., pp. iii-iv.

[99] Ibid., p. vi.

[100] Ibid., pp. v – vi.

[101] Ibid., p. vii.

[102] DHS, *Comprehensive Biometric Air Exit Plan, Fiscal Year 2012 Report to Congress*, Washington, DC, May 11, 2012, pp. 3-4.

[103] H-2A visas permit certain foreign workers to perform temporary nonagricultural service or labor, and H-2B visas permit certain foreign workers to perform non-agricultural service or labor; see CRS Report R42434, *Immigration of Temporary Lower-Skilled Workers: Current Policy and Related Issues*, by Andorra Bruno.

[104] GAO-10-13, p. 19.

[105] GAO, *Overstay Enforcement: Additional Mechanisms for Collecting, Assessing, and Sharing Data Could Strengthen DHS's Efforts but Would Have Costs*, GAO-11-411, April 2011, p. 11.

[106] DHS briefing for CRS, April 3, 2013.

[107] The Senate-passed Border Security, Economic Opportunity, and Immigration Modernization Act (S. 744) would require air carriers to collect machine readable exit data from departing passengers. Some have argued that a machine readable system would be more secure. For example, in the wake of the Boston Marathon bombing, some people hypothesized that the manual input of passenger name information contributed to alleged bomber Tamerlan Tsarnaev's ability, after previously being investigated by the FBI, to travel back and forth to Russia without triggering additional scrutiny, though it appears that his travel did generate a "hit" against certain passenger name checks.

[108] For a fuller discussion, see CRS Report 96-397, *Canada-U.S. Relations*.

[109] Canada Border Services Agency (CBSA) and DHS, "Entry/Exit Information System Phase I Joint Canada-United States Report," May 8, 2013.

[110] CBSA, "Entry Exit Initiative – Phase II Privacy Impact Assessment (PIA) Executive Summary," June 28, 2013.

[111] DHS briefing for CRS, April 3, 2013; also see Testimony of DHS Assistant Secretary David Heyman, U.S. Congress, House Committee on Judiciary, *Implementation of an Entry-Exit System: Still Waiting After All These Years*, 113th Cong., 1st sess., November 13, 2013. Hereafter: Heyman Testimony, 2013.

[112] GAO, *Overstay Enforcement: Additional Actions Needed to Assess DHS's Data and Improve Planning for a Biometric Air Exit Program*, GAO-13-683, July 2013, pp. 12-14.

[113] Ibid., pp. 16-18.

[114] Testimony of DHS Secretary Janet Napolitano, U.S. Congress, Senate Committee on the Judiciary, *Comprehensive Immigration Reform*, 113th Cong., 1st sess., February 13, 2013. Hereafter: Napolitano testimony, 2013.

[115] See Ibid.

[116] ICE's main program to apprehend at-large removable aliens in the United States is the National Fugitive Operations Program (NFOP), which mainly focuses on at-large criminal aliens and fugitive aliens, including but not limited to high-priority visa overstayers. The NFOP consisted of 129 fugitive operations teams as of July 2013, and was responsible for 37,371 arrests in FY2012. See CRS Report R42057, *Interior Immigration Enforcement: Programs Targeting Criminal Aliens*.

[117] Heyman Testimony, 2013.

[118] CBP, Secure Borders, Safe Travel, Legal Trade: Fiscal Year 2009-2014 Strategic Plan, CBP, Washington, DC, 2009, p. 15.

[119] See for example Testimony of CBP Deputy Assistant Commissioner John Wagner, U.S. Congress, House Committee on Oversight and Government Affairs, Subcommittee on National Security, *Border Security Oversight, Part III: Border Crossing Cards and B1/B2 Visas*, 113th Cong., 1st sess., November 14, 2013.

[120] For a fuller discussion, see CRS Report R43097, *Comprehensive Immigration Reform in the 113th Congress: Major Provisions in Senate-Passed S. 744*.

[121] S. 744 § 1201.

[122] For a fuller discussion, see CRS Report R43320, *Immigration Legislation and Issues in the 113th Congress*.

[123] Pew Hispanic Center, "Fact Sheet: Modes of Entry for the Unauthorized Migrant Population," Pew Hispanic Center, Washington, DC, May 22, 2006. Also see CRS Report RS22446, *Nonimmigrant Overstays: Brief Synthesis of the Issue*.

[124] Jonathan Hicken, Mollie Cohen, and Jorge Narvaez, "Double Jeopardy: How U.S. Enforcement Policies Shape Tunkaseño Migration," in *Mexican Migration and the U.S. Economic Crisis*, ed. Wayne A. Cornelius, David FitzGerald, Pedro Lewin Fischer, and Leah Muse-Orlinoff (La Jolla, CA: University of California, San Diego Center for Comparative Immigration Studies, 2010), pp-60-61 and CRS communication with the authors.

[125] Napolitano testimony, 2013.

[126] According to CBP Office of Congressional Affairs (communication with CRS, December 30, 2013), CBP believes that developing a reliable estimate of unauthorized inflows at POEs would require substantially increasing the COMPEX sample size and would have a direct negative impact on secondary delays and wait times. The department told CRS that the necessary expansion in officer time, training costs, and technology devoted to COMPEX inspections would be cost and time prohibitive at many busy ports, and would be counterproductive to the mission of the agency.

[127] A similar argument can be made about the relationship among POE infrastructure and personnel, trade facilitation, and security; see CRS Report R43014, *U.S. Customs and Border Protection: Trade Facilitation, Enforcement, and Security*. The benefits of adding infrastructure and personnel may be greatest when such increases coincide, in order to maintain an effective ratio of agents per lane.

[128] GAO, *Border Security: Despite Progress, Weaknesses in Traveler Inspections Exist at Our Nations Ports of Entry*, GAO-08-329T, January 3, 2008, pp. 7-9.

[129] GAO, *Border Security: DHS Progress and Challenges in Securing the U.S. Southwest and Northern Borders*, GAO-11-508T, March 30, 2011, pp. 5-6.

[130] CBP Office of Congressional Affairs, January 8, 2014.

[131] DHS, CBP Salaries and Expenses Congressional Budget Justification, FY2014, p. 18.

[132] CBP's Office of Field Operations is responsible for enforcement at ports of entry (POEs); the Border Patrol is responsible for enforcement between POEs; and Immigration and Customs Enforcement is responsible for immigration enforcement within the United States and for customs-related investigations.

[133] According to the Congressional Research Service's (CRS) analysis of CBP data, CBP officer staffing on the Southwest border increased 35% between 2004 (the first year for which data are available) and 2013, from 4,771 to 6,444 officers. During the same period, Border Patrol personnel on the Southwest border increased 94%, from 9,506 to 18,462 agents. For a fuller discussion, see CRS General Distribution memorandum, "Immigration Enforcement Since 2006," by Marc R. Rosenblum, available to congressional clients from the author.

[134] Section 1102 of S. 744 would require DHS to deploy 38,405 Border Patrol agents to the Southwest border, up from about 18,500 in FY2013, and would require CBP to add 3,500 OFO officers nationwide, up from about 21,800 in FY2013.

[135] See for example, the Putting Our Resources Toward Security (PORTS) Act (H.R. 583), the Cross-Border Trade Enhancement act of 2013 (H.R. 1108/S. 178), and the Emergency Port of Entry Personnel and Infrastructure Funding Act of 2013 (H.R. 3753/S. 1812).

[136] For a fuller discussion, see CRS Report R43147, *Department of Homeland Security: FY2014 Appropriations*.

[137] See section 560 of the Consolidated and Further Continuing Appropriations Act, 2013 (P.L. 113-6, Div. D). The pilot program currently permits five such partnerships in Dallas, TX, Houston, TX, and Miami, FL and land POEs in El Paso, TX and Laredo/McAllen, TX.

[138] The Obama Administration proposed expanding the PPP program in its FY2014 Budget Justification. The Senate Appropriations Committee Report (S.Rept. 113-77) supports the Administration's proposal, but the House Appropriations Committee Report (H.Rept. 113-91) does not. In addition, section 411 of the Trade Facilitation and Trade Enforcement Reauthorization Act of 2013 (S. 662) would repeal the PPP pilot program.

[139] CBP also uses trusted trade programs as a risk management tool for commercial flows; see CRS Report R43014, *U.S. Customs and Border Protection: Trade Facilitation, Enforcement, and Security*.

[140] See for example the Jobs Originated through Launching Travel (JOLT) Act of 2013 (H.R. 1354).

[141] See U.S. Department of Commerce, *Draft Report: Improving Economic Outcomes by Reducing Border Delays, Facilitating the Vital Flow of Commercial Traffic Across the US-Mexican Border*, Washington, DC, 2008.

In: Immigration Inspections and Enforcement ...   ISBN: 978-1-63117-409-4
Editor: Marcella Magdalena   © 2014 Nova Science Publishers, Inc.

Chapter 2

BORDER SECURITY: IMMIGRATION ENFORCEMENT BETWEEN PORTS OF ENTRY[*]

Marc R. Rosenblum

SUMMARY

Border enforcement is a core element of the Department of Homeland Security's (DHS's) effort to control unauthorized migration, with the U.S. Border Patrol (USBP) within the Bureau of Customs and Border Protection (CBP) as the lead agency along most of the border. Border enforcement has been an ongoing subject of congressional interest since the 1970s, when illegal immigration to the United States first registered as a serious national problem; and border security has received additional attention in the years since the terrorist attacks of 2001.

Since the 1990s, migration control at the border has been guided by a strategy of "prevention through deterrence"—the idea that the concentration of personnel, infrastructure, and surveillance technology along heavily trafficked regions of the border will discourage unauthorized aliens from attempting to enter the United States. Since 2005, CBP has attempted to discourage repeat entries and disrupt migrant smuggling networks by imposing tougher penalties against certain unauthorized aliens, a set of policies eventually described as

---

[*] This is an edited, reformatted and augmented version of Congressional Research Service Publication, No. R42138, dated May 3, 2013.

"enforcement with consequences." Most people apprehended at the Southwest border are now subject to "high consequence" enforcement outcomes.

Across a variety of indicators, the United States has substantially expanded border enforcement resources over the last three decades. Particularly since 2001, such increases include border security appropriations, personnel, fencing and infrastructure, and surveillance technology.

The Border Patrol collects data on several different border enforcement outcomes; and this report describes trends in border apprehensions, recidivism, and estimated got aways and turn backs. Yet none of these existing data are designed to measure illegal border flows or the degree to which the border is secured. Thus, the report also describes methods for estimating illegal border flows based on enforcement data and migrant surveys.

Drawing on multiple data sources, the report suggests conclusions about the state of border security. Robust investments at the border were not associated with reduced illegal inflows during the 1980s and 1990s, but a range of evidence suggests a substantial drop in illegal inflows in 2007-2011, followed by a slight rise in 2012. Enforcement, along with the economic downturn in the United States, likely contributed to the drop in unauthorized migration, though the precise share of the decline attributable to enforcement is unknown.

Enhanced border enforcement also may have contributed to a number of secondary costs and benefits. To the extent that border enforcement successfully deters illegal entries, such enforcement may reduce border-area violence and migrant deaths, protect fragile border ecosystems, and improve the quality of life in border communities. But to the extent that aliens are not deterred, the concentration of enforcement resources on the border may increase border area violence and migrant deaths, encourage unauthorized migrants to find new ways to enter illegally and to remain in the United States for longer periods of time, damage border ecosystems, harm border-area businesses and the quality of life in border communities, and strain U.S. relations with Mexico and Canada.

INTRODUCTION

The country's immigration and naturalization laws have been subjects of episodic controversy since America's founding, but *illegal* immigration only became an issue in the early 20th century, when Congress passed the first strict restrictions on legal admissions. Illegal immigration declined during the Great Depression and during and after World War II, when most labor migration occurred through the U.S.-Mexico Bracero program.[1] Immigration control re-emerged as a national concern during the 1970s, when the end of the Bracero program, new restrictions on Western Hemisphere migration, and growing U.S. demand for foreign-born workers combined to cause a sharp increase in unauthorized migration flows.[2]

Congress responded in 1986 by passing the Immigration Reform and Control Act (IRCA, P.L. 99 603), which authorized a 50% increase in Border Patrol staffing, among other provisions. Border security[3] has remained a persistent topic of congressional interest since then, and enforcement programs and appropriations have grown accordingly, as described in this report.

Despite a growing enforcement response, however, illegal immigration continued to increase over most of the next three decades, with the estimated unauthorized population peaking at 12 million-12.4 million people in 2007.[4] Unauthorized migration has declined since 2007, with the estimated unauthorized population falling to 11.1 million-11.5 million in 2011.[5] Apprehensions of unauthorized migrants at the U.S.-Mexico border fell from about 1.2 million in 2005 to a 41-year low of 328,000 in 2011, before climbing slightly to 357,000 in 2012.[6]

The Obama Administration cites falling apprehensions, among other statistics, as evidence that the border is more secure than ever.[7] Yet some Members of Congress and others disagree and have called on the Administration to do more to secure the border. Border security has been a recurrent theme in Congress's debate about comprehensive immigration reform since 2005, and some Members of Congress have argued that Congress should not consider additional immigration reforms until the border is more secure.[8]

This report reviews efforts to combat unauthorized migration across the Southwest border in the nearly three decades since IRCA initiated the modern era in migration control, takes stock of the current state of border security, and considers lessons that may be learned about enhanced enforcement at U.S. borders. The report begins by reviewing the history of border control and the development of a national border control strategy beginning in the 1990s. The following sections summarize appropriations and resources dedicated to border enforcement, indicators of enforcement outcomes, metrics for estimating unauthorized migration flows, and possible secondary and unintended consequences of border enforcement. The report concludes by reviewing the overall costs and benefits of the current approach to migration control and raising additional questions that may help guide the discussion of these issues in the future.

BORDER PATROL HISTORY AND STRATEGY

Congress created the U.S. Border Patrol (USBP) within the Department of Commerce and Labor by an appropriations act in 1924,[9] two days after passing the first permanent numeric immigration restrictions.[10] Numerical limits only applied to the Eastern Hemisphere, barring most Asian immigration; and the Border Patrol's initial focus was on preventing the entry of Chinese migrants, as well as combating gun trafficking and alcohol imports during prohibition. The majority of agents were stationed on the northern border.[11] The Border Patrol became part of the new Immigration and Naturalization Service (INS) in 1933, and the INS moved from the Department of Labor to the Department of Justice in 1940. The Border Patrol's focus shifted to the Southwest border during World War II, but preventing illegal migration across the Southwest border remained a low priority during most of the 20th century.[12]

Illegal migration from Mexico increased after 1965 as legislative changes restricted legal Mexican immigration at the same time that social and economic changes caused stronger migration "pushes" in Mexico (e.g., inadequate employment opportunities) and stronger "pulls" in the United States (e.g., employment opportunities, links to migrant communities in Mexico).[13] Congress held hearings on illegal immigration beginning in 1971, and after more than a decade of debate passed the Immigration Reform and Control Act of 1986 (IRCA, P.L. 99-603), which described border enforcement as an "essential element" of immigration control and, as mentioned, authorized a 50% increase in funding for the Border Patrol, among other provisions.[14]

Congress passed at least 11 additional laws addressing illegal immigration over the next two decades, seven of which included provisions related to the border.[15]

Border Patrol Strategic Plans

Seventy years after it began operations, the Border Patrol developed its first formal national border control strategy in 1994, the National Strategic Plan. The plan was updated in 2004 and again in 2012.

National Strategic Plan
The National Strategic Plan (NSP) was developed in 1994 in response to a widespread perception that the Southwest border was being overrun by

unauthorized immigration and drug smuggling, and to respond to a study commissioned by the Office of National Drug Control Policy. The study recommended that the INS change its approach from arresting unauthorized immigrants after they enter the United States, as had previously been the case, to focus instead on preventing their entry.[16] Under the new approach, the INS would place personnel, surveillance technology, fencing, and other infrastructure directly on the border to discourage illegal flows, a strategy that became known as "prevention through deterrence." According to the 1994 INS plan, "the prediction is that with traditional entry and smuggling routes disrupted, illegal traffic will be deterred, or forced over more hostile terrain, less suited for crossing and more suited for enforcement."[17]

The NSP described a multi-phased approach with Phase I including the "Hold the Line" program in El Paso, TX, and Operation Gatekeeper in San Diego, CA.[18] Phase II included the expansion of Operation Rio Grande (1997) in the McAllen and Laredo sectors of Texas and Operation Safeguard (1999) in Tucson, AZ. Phases III and IV were to involve the remaining areas of the Southwest border followed by the Gulf Coast and Northern borders.[19]

The implementation of Phase II and subsequent phases was to be based on the success of Phase I, with the plan describing several expected indicators of effective border enforcement, including an initial increase of border arrests and entry attempt to be followed by an eventual reduction of arrests, a change in traditional traffic patterns, and an increase in more sophisticated smuggling methods.[20] As predicted, apprehensions within the San Diego and El Paso sectors fell sharply beginning in 1994-1995, and traffic patterns shifted, primarily to the Tucson and South Texas (Rio Grande Valley) sectors (see "Southwest Border Apprehensions by Sector"). A 1997 General Accounting Office (GAO) report was cautiously optimistic about the strategy.[21]

Congress supported the prevention through deterrence approach. In 1996, House and Senate appropriators directed the INS to hire new agents and to reallocate personnel from the interior to front line duty.[22] And the Illegal Immigration Reform and Immigrant Responsibility Act of 1996 (P.L. 104-208) expressly authorized the construction and improvement of fencing and other barriers along the Southwest border and required the completion of a triple-layered fence along 14 miles of the border near San Diego where the INS had begun to install fencing in 1990.[23]

National Border Patrol Strategy

In the wake of the 9/11 attacks, the USBP refocused its priorities on preventing terrorist penetration, while remaining committed to its traditional duties of preventing the illicit trafficking of people and contraband between official ports of entry. Shortly after the creation of DHS, USBP was directed to formulate a new National Border Patrol Strategy (NBPS) that would better reflect the realities of the post-9/11 security landscape. In March 2004, the Border Patrol unveiled the National Border Patrol Strategy, which placed greater emphasis on interdicting terrorists and featured five main objectives:

- establishing the substantial probability of apprehending terrorists and their weapons as they attempt to enter illegally between the ports of entry;
- deterring illegal entries through improved enforcement;
- detecting, apprehending, and deterring smugglers of humans, drugs, and other contraband;
- leveraging "Smart Border" technology to multiply the deterrent and enforcement effect of agents; and
- reducing crime in border communities, thereby improving the quality of life and economic vitality of those areas.[24]

The NBPS was an attempt to lay the foundation for achieving "operational control" over the border, defined by the Border Patrol as "the ability to detect, respond, and interdict border penetrations in areas deemed as high priority for threat potential or other national security objectives."[25] The strategy emphasized a hierarchical and vertical command structure, featuring a direct chain of command from headquarters to the field. The document emphasized the use of tactical, operational, and strategic intelligence and sophisticated surveillance systems to assess risk and target enforcement efforts; and the rapid deployment of USBP agents to respond to emerging threats. Additionally, the plan called for the Border Patrol to coordinate closely with CBP's Office of Intelligence and other federal intelligence agencies.

Border Patrol Strategic Plan

CBP published a new Border Patrol Strategic Plan (BPSP) in May 2012 that shifted attention from resource acquisition and deployment to the strategic allocation of resources by "focusing enhanced capabilities against the highest threats and rapidly responding along the border."[26] From an operational perspective, the 2012 plan emphasizes the collection and analysis of information about evolving border threats; integration of Border Patrol and CBP planning across different border sectors and among the full range of federal, state, local, tribal, and international organizations involved in border security operations; and rapid Border Patrol response to specific border threats.[27]

DHS Secure Border Initiative

The Border Patrol's approach to border enforcement has been mirrored in broader DHS policies. In November 2005, the Department of Homeland Security announced a comprehensive multiyear plan, the Secure Border Initiative (SBI), to secure U.S. borders and reduce illegal migration.[28] Under SBI, DHS announced plans to obtain operational control of the northern and southern borders within five years by focusing attention in five main areas:

- **Increased staffing**. As part of SBI, DHS announced the addition of 1,000 new Border Patrol agents, 250 new ICE investigators targeting human smuggling operations, and 500 other new ICE agents and officers.[29]
- **Improved detention and removal capacity**. Historically, most non-Mexicans apprehended at the border were placed in formal removal proceedings.[30] Yet backlogs in the immigration court system meant that most such aliens were released on bail or on their own recognizance prior to a removal hearing, and many failed to show up for their hearings.[31] In October 2005, DHS announced plans to detain 100% of non-Mexicans apprehended at the border until they could be processed for removal. SBI supported this goal by adding detention capacity, initially increasing bed space by 2,000 to a total of 20,000.[32] On August 23, 2006, DHS announced that the policy to "end catch and release" had been successfully implemented.[33]
- **Surveillance technology**. SBI included plans to expand DHS' use of surveillance technology between ports of entry, including unmanned aerial vehicle (UAV) systems, other aerial assets, remote video surveillance (RVS) systems, and ground sensors.[34] These tools were to be linked into a common integrated system that became known as SBI*net* (see "**Surveillance Assets**" below).
- **Tactical infrastructure**. SBI continued DHS' commitment to the expansion of border fencing, roads, and stadium-style lighting.[35]
- **Interior enforcement**. SBI also included plans to expand enforcement within the United States at worksites and through state

and local partnerships, jail screening programs, and task forces to locate fugitive aliens.[36]

CBP Consequence Delivery System

Although not the subject of a formal public policy document like those discussed above, an additional component of CBP's approach to border control in recent years has been an effort to promote "high consequence" enforcement for unauthorized Mexicans apprehended at the border.[37] Historically, immigration agents permitted most Mexicans apprehended at the border to voluntarily return to Mexico without any penalty.[38] Since 2005, CBP has limited voluntary returns in favor of three types of "high consequence" outcomes:

- **Formal Removal**.[39] Aliens[40] formally removed from the United States generally are ineligible for a visa (i.e., inadmissible) for at least five years,[41] and they may be subject to criminal charges if they illegally reenter the United States.[42] Prior to 2005, most unauthorized Mexicans apprehended at the border were not placed in removal proceedings, in part because standard removal procedures require an appearance before an immigration judge and are resource intensive. Since 2005, CBP has relied extensively on two provisions in the Immigration and Nationality Act (INA) that permit aliens to be formally removed with limited judicial processing. Under INA §235(b), certain arriving aliens are subject to "expedited removal" (ER) without additional hearing or review.[43] ER was added to the INA in 1996, but initially was reserved for aliens apprehended at ports of entry. In a series of four announcements between November 2002 and January 2006, DHS expanded the use of ER to include certain aliens who had entered the United States within the previous two weeks and who were apprehended anywhere within 100 miles of a U.S. land or coastal border.[44] Under INA §241(a)(5), an alien who reenters the United States after being formally removed or departing under a removal order is subject to "reinstatement of removal" without reopening or reviewing the original removal order.[45]
- **Criminal Charges**. Unauthorized aliens apprehended at the border may face federal immigration charges,[46] but historically, most have not been charged with a crime. Working with the Department of

Justice (DOJ), DHS has increased the proportion of people apprehended at the border who are charged with immigration-related criminal offenses. About half of aliens facing criminal charges in Southwest border districts are prosecuted through the "Operation Streamline" program (see accompanying text box). Mexicans apprehended in the United States who are found to be smuggling aliens may also be subject to criminal charges in Mexico under the U.S.-Mexican Operation Against Smugglers Initiative on Safety and Security (OASISS).[47]

- **Remote repatriation**. CBP uses a pair of programs to return Mexicans to remote locations rather than to the nearest Mexican port of entry. Under the Alien Transfer Exit Program (ATEP), certain Mexicans apprehended near the border are repatriated to border ports hundreds of miles away—typically moving people from Arizona to Texas or California—a process commonly described as "lateral repatriation."[48] Under the Mexican Interior Repatriation Program (MIRP), certain Mexican nationals are repatriated to their home towns within Mexico rather than being returned just across the border.[49]

Operation Streamline

Operation Streamline is a partnership program among CBP, U.S. Attorneys, and District Court judges in certain border districts to expedite criminal justice processing. The program permits groups of up to 40 criminal defendants to have their cases heard at the same time, rather than requiring judges to review individual charges, and arranges in most cases for aliens facing felony charges for illegal re-entry to plead guilty to misdemeanor illegal entry charges—a plea bargain that leads to the rapid resolution of cases. Although Operation Streamline has been described as a zero tolerance program leading to prosecutions for 100% of apprehended aliens, the program confronts limits in judicial and detention capacity, resulting in daily caps on the number of people facing charges in certain districts. In the Tucson sector, for example, the courts reportedly limit Streamline cases to about 70 prosecutions per day.

Operation Streamline was established in the USBP's Del Rio Sector in December 2005 and expanded to the Yuma Sector in December 2006, Laredo Sector in October 2007, Tucson Sector in January 2008, and Rio Grande Valley Sector in June 2008.

The program mainly consists of procedural arrangements among DHS and DOJ officials at the local level, and 15 CBP agents have been detailed to DOJ in three Border Patrol sectors to assist DOJ attorneys and U.S. Marshalls with prosecutions. A total of 208,939 people were processed through Operation Streamline through the end of FY2012—about 45% of the 463,051 immigration-related prosecutions in Southwest border districts during this period.

Sources: CBP Office of Congressional Affairs; National Research Council Committee on Estimating Costs of Immigration Enforcement in the Department of Justice, *Budgeting for Immigration Enforcement: A Path to Better Performance* (Washington, DC: National Academies Press, 2011).

In general, these high consequence enforcement outcomes are intended to deter illegal flows by raising the costs to migrants of being apprehended and by making it more difficult for them to reconnect with smugglers following a failed entry attempt.[50] To manage these disparate programs, CBP has designed the "Consequence Delivery System... to uniquely evaluate each subject [who is apprehended] and identify the ideal consequences to deliver to impede and deter further illegal activity."[51] USBP agents use laminated cards with matrices describing the range of enforcement actions available for a particular alien as a function of the person's immigration and criminal histories, among other factors, and of the enforcement resources available in each Border Patrol sector. According to public comments by then CBP Commissioner Alan Bersin, the goal of the Consequence Delivery System, in certain sectors of the border, is to ensure that virtually everyone who is apprehended faces "some type of consequence" other than voluntary return.[52]

As **Figure 1** indicates, the effort to limit voluntary returns in favor of "high consequence" enforcement outcomes has, to a great degree, been implemented. The figure depicts Southwest border apprehensions (the solid line) and the four main types of enforcement outcomes (voluntary returns, criminal charges, formal removal, and remote repatriation—the shaded areas) for FY2005-FY2012. (Enforcement outcomes exceed apprehensions because some aliens face more than one outcome, such as formal removal along with lateral repatriation. In addition, certain aliens apprehended in one fiscal year do not complete their case processing until the following year.) As the figure illustrates, voluntary return fell from 77% of all enforcement outcomes in 2005 (956,470 out of 1,238,554) to 14% in FY2012 (76,664 out of 529,393). Conversely, the proportion of enforcement outcomes that were high consequence outcomes (i.e., criminal charges, formal removal, or remote repatriation) increased from 23% (282,084 out of 1,238,554) in FY2005 to 86% in FY2012 (452,664 out of 529,393).

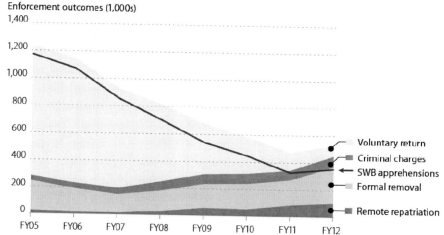

Sources: CRS presentation of data provided by CBP Office of Congressional Affairs March 10, 2013; ICE Office of Congressional Affairs March 22, 2013; Administrative Office of the U.S. Courts.

Notes: Immigration-related criminal charges may include some U.S. citizens and lawful aliens.

Figure 1. CBP "Enforcement with Consequences," FY2005-FY2012; Southwest Border.

One factor that has facilitated the rise in the proportion of apprehensions subject to high-consequence enforcement has been a sharp drop in the number of aliens apprehended on the Southwest border, as discussed in this report (see **"Alien Apprehensions"**). Nonetheless, as **Figure 1** also illustrates, CBP's effort to expand high-consequence enforcement has resulted in an *absolute* rise in removals, prosecutions, and lateral/interior repatriations since 2007, even during a period of falling border apprehensions.

With the implementation of the Consequence Delivery System, the Border Patrol has initiated a new system to estimate the deterrent effect of different enforcement outcomes. In particular, USBP tracks, for each of 10 different enforcement consequences, the percentage of aliens who were re-apprehended during the same fiscal year following repatriation (i.e., the recidivism rate). These recidivism rates are reported in **Table 1**.

Table 1. Consequence Delivery System Outcomes and Recidivism Rates; Southwest Border

Consequence		FY2011		FY2012	
		Number of Cases	Recidivism Rate	Number of Cases	Recidivism Rate
Criminal Charges	OASISS	533	14.7%	429	10.2%
	Operation Streamline	36,871	12.1%	44,300	10.3%
	Standard Prosecution	31,130	9.1%	34,839	9.1%
Formal Removal	Notice to Appear	20,923	6.6%	23,491	3.8%
	Expedited Removal	39,855	16.6%	148,548	16.4%
	Reinstatement	74,106	16.9%	98,424	15.9%
	Quick Court	2,730	19.0%	1,070	18.3%
Remote Repatriation	MIRP	8,940	9.3%	0	NA[a]
	ATEP	75,966	27.8%	101,992	23.8%
Voluntary Return		129,207	29.4%	76,664	27.1%
Total Cases		318,883	19.8%	347,921	16.7%

Source: CRS analysis based on data provided by CBP Office of Congressional Affairs, March 10, 2013.

Notes: OASISS stands for the U.S.-Mexican Operation Against Smugglers Initiative on Safety and Security. See text for discussions of Operation Streamline, expedited removal, and reinstatement of removal. Standard Prosecution refers to criminal charges through the standard federal prosecution process. Notice to appear is the first stage in the standard formal removal process before an immigration judge. Quick court is a program involving expedited removal hearings before an immigration judge. MIRP stands for the Mexico Interior Repatriation Program. ATEP stands for the Alien Transfer Exchange Program. Total Cases refers to the total number of apprehensions and border-wide overall recidivism rate. The sum of the consequences exceeds the number of total cases because some people are subject to more than one consequence.

[a] MIRP did not operate in FY2012.

As **Table 1** indicates, several consequences were associated with recidivism rates well *below* the overall FY2012 average of 16.7%. These low recidivism consequences included standard removal proceedings following a notice to appear (3.8%), standard criminal prosecutions (9.1%), criminal charges through the OASISS program (10.2%), and Operation Streamline (10.3%). Recidivism rates were also lower than the FY2011 average of 19.8% for aliens returned to Mexico through the MIRP program (9.3%) in that year.

(MIRP did not operate in FY2012.) Conversely, recidivism rates in FY2012 were well *above* the overall average for aliens subject to voluntary return (27.1%) and for aliens subject to lateral repatriation through the ATEP program (23.8%).

The differences in recidivism rates may not be wholly attributable to differences among the consequences because the Border Patrol takes account of aliens' migration histories and other factors when assigning people to different enforcement outcomes. Nonetheless, these data suggest that standard removal and criminal charges have a stronger deterrent effect on future unauthorized migration than does voluntary return. Conversely, lateral repatriation appears to do little to discourage people from reentering the United States.[53]

BUDGET AND RESOURCES

Statutory and strategic changes since 1986 are reflected in border enforcement appropriations and in CBP's assets at the border, including personnel, infrastructure, and surveillance technology. This section reviews trends in each of these areas.

Border Security Appropriations

Figure 2 depicts U.S. Border Patrol appropriations for FY1989-FY2013. Appropriations have grown steadily over this period, rising from $232 million in 1989 to $1.3 billion in FY2002 (the last data available prior to the creation of DHS), $3.8 billion in FY2010, and $3.7 billion in FY2013—a nominal increase of 1,450% and an increase of 730% when accounting for inflation.[54] The largest growth came following the formation of DHS in FY2003, reflecting Congress's focus on border security in the aftermath of 9/11.

Appropriations reported in **Figure 2** are only a *subset* of all border security funding. These data do not include, for example, additional CBP sub-accounts funding Headquarters Management and Administration ($1.4 billion in FY2013), and Border Security Inspections and Trade Facilitation at Ports of Entry ($3.2 billion); or additional CBP accounts funding Border Security Fencing, Infrastructure, and Technology ($324 million); Air and Marine Operations ($799 million) and Construction and Facilities Management ($234 million).[55]

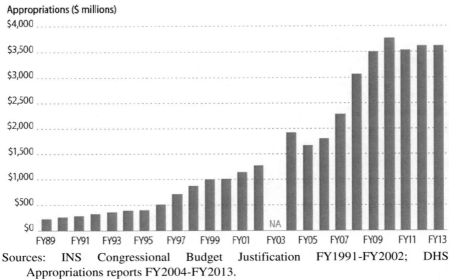

Sources: INS   Congressional   Budget   Justification   FY1991-FY2002;   DHS
    Appropriations reports FY2004-FY2013.
Notes: Appropriations for 1989-2002 reflect the "Border Patrol" sub-account of the
    INS   Salaries   and   Expenses   account   of   the   DOJ   annual   appropriations.
    Appropriations for 2004-2012 reflect the "Border Security and Control between
    Ports of Entry" sub-account of the CBP Salaries and Expenses account of the
    DHS annual appropriations. Data are not available for FY2003 because neither the
    INS nor congressional appropriators provided a breakout of the salaries and
    expenses sub-accounts within the Enforcement and Border Affairs account during
    that year's funding cycle. The overall Enforcement and Border Affairs account
    within INS for FY2003 was $2,881 million, up from $2,541 million in FY2001
    and $2,740 million in FY2002. With the establishment of DHS, the former INS,
    customs inspections from the former U.S. Customs Service, and the U.S. Border
    Patrol were merged to form the Bureau of Customs and Border Protection within
    DHS. As a result, data for years prior to FY2003 may not be strictly comparable
    with data for FY2004 and after. FY2005 figure includes a $124 million
    supplemental appropriation from P.L. 109-13. FY2006 figure does not include any
    portion of the $423 million in supplemental funding for CBP Salaries and
    Expenses in P.L. 109-234 because the law did not specify how much of this
    funding was for USBP; DHS reported in its FY2008 DHS Budget Justification
    that the Border Patrol received a $1,900 million appropriation in FY2006. FY2010
    figure includes a $176 million supplemental appropriation from P.L. 111-230.

Figure 2. U.S. Border Patrol Appropriations, FY1989-FY2013.

A substantial portion of these accounts is dedicated to border security and immigration enforcement, as these terms are commonly used. The data in **Figure 2** also exclude U.S. Immigration and Customs Enforcement (ICE) appropriations, which totaled $5.4 billion for Salaries and Expenses for FY2013.[56] About a quarter of ICE's 20,000 personnel reportedly are deployed to the Southwest border.[57] And **Figure 2** excludes border enforcement appropriations for other federal agencies—including the Departments of Justice, Defense, the Interior, and Agriculture, all of which play a role in border security—as well as funding for the U.S. federal court system.[58]

Border Patrol Personnel

Accompanying this budget increase, Congress has passed at least four laws since 1986 authorizing increased Border Patrol personnel.[59] USBP staffing roughly doubled in the decade after the 1986 IRCA, doubled again between 1996 and the 9/11 attacks, and doubled again in the decade after 9/11 (see **Figure 3**). As of January 2013, the USBP had 21,370 agents, including 18,462 posted at the Southwest border and 2,212 posted at the northern border.[60] These numbers are up from a total of 2,268 Border Patrol agents in 1980 (including 1,975 at the Southwest border and 211 at the northern border) and 10,045 in 2002 (including 9,239 at the Southwest border and 492 at the northern border).[61]

National Guard Troops at the Border

The National Guard also is authorized to support federal, state, and local law enforcement agencies (LEAs) at the border. Basic authority for the Department of Defense (DOD, including the National Guard) to assist LEAs is contained in Chapter 18 of Title 10 of the U.S. Code, and DOD personnel are expressly authorized to maintain and operate equipment in cooperation with federal LEAs in conjunction with the enforcement of counterterrorism operations or the enforcement of counterdrug laws, immigration laws, and customs requirements.[62] DOD may assist any federal, state, or local LEA requesting counterdrug assistance under the National Defense Authorization Act, as amended.[63] Under Title 32 of the U.S. Code, National Guard personnel also may serve a federal purpose, such as border security, and receive federal pay while remaining under the command control of their respective state governors.[64]

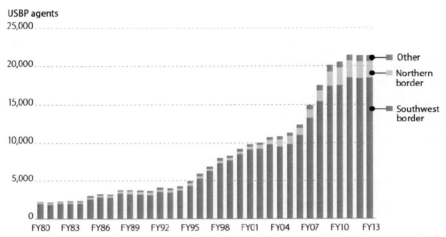

Source: 1980-1991: CRS presentation of data from Syracuse University Transactional
    Records Access Clearinghouse; 1992-2011: CRS presentation of data provided by
    CBP Office of Congressional Affairs.
Note: The total number of Border Patrol agents includes agents stationed in coastal
    sectors and at USBP headquarters.

Figure 3. U.S. Border Patrol Agents, Total and by Region, FY1980-FY2013.

National Guard troops were first deployed to the border on a pilot basis in
1988, when about 100 soldiers assisted the U.S. Customs Service at several
Southwest border locations, and National Guard and active military units
provided targeted support for the USBP's surveillance programs throughout
the following decade. The first large-scale deployment of the National Guard
to the border occurred in 2006-2008, when over 30,000 troops provided
engineering, aviation, identification, technical, logistical, and administrative
support to CBP as part of "Operation Jump Start."[65] President Obama
announced an additional deployment of up to 1,200 National Guard troops to
the Southwest border on May 25, 2010, with the National Guard supporting
the Border Patrol, by providing intelligence work and drug and human
trafficking interdiction.[66] The 2010 deployment was originally scheduled to
end in June 2011, but the full deployment was extended twice (in June and
September 2011). The Administration announced in December 2011 that the
deployment would be reduced to fewer than 300 troops beginning in January
2012, with National Guard efforts focused on supporting DHS's aerial
surveillance operations.[67] In December 2012, DHS and the Department of

Defense announced that the National Guard deployment would be extended through December 2013.[68]

Fencing and Tactical Infrastructure

Border tactical infrastructure includes roads, lighting, pedestrian fencing, and vehicle barriers. Tactical infrastructure is intended to impede illicit cross-border activity, disrupt and restrict smuggling operations, and establish a substantial probability of apprehending terrorists seeking entry into the United States.[69] The former INS installed the first fencing along the U.S.-Mexican border beginning in 1990 east of the Pacific Ocean near San Diego.

Congress expressly authorized the construction and improvement of fencing and other barriers under Section 102(a) of the Illegal Immigration Reform and Immigrant Responsibility Act of 1996 (IIRIRA; P.L. 104-208, Div. C), which also required (pursuant to Section 102(b)) the completion of a triple-layered fence along the original 14 mile border segment near San Diego. The Secure Fence Act of 2006 (P.L. 109-367) amended IIRIRA Section 102(b) with a requirement for double-layered fencing along five segments of the Southwest border, totaling about 850 miles.[70] IIRIRA was amended again by the Consolidated Appropriations Act, FY2008 (P.L. 110- 161). Under that amendment, the law now requires the Secretary of Homeland Security to construct reinforced fencing "along not less than 700 miles of the southwest border where fencing would be most practical and effective and provide for the installation of additional physical barriers, roads, lighting, cameras, and sensors to gain operational control of the southwest border."[71] The act further specifies, however, that the Secretary of Homeland Security is *not* required to install fencing "in a particular location along the international border of the United States if the Secretary determines that the use or placement of such resources is not the most appropriate means to achieve and maintain operational control over the international border at such location."[72]

As of January 15, 2013, DHS had installed 352 miles of primary pedestrian fencing, 299 miles of vehicle fencing (total of 651 miles), and 36 miles of secondary fencing (see **Figure 4**). The Border Patrol reportedly had identified a total of 653 miles of the border as appropriate for fencing and barriers (i.e., 2 additional miles).[73] **Figure 4** also summarizes annual appropriations for tactical infrastructure (including surveillance technology) for FY1996-FY2013. Appropriations increased from $25 million in FY1996 to $298 million in FY2006, an eleven-fold increase (eight-fold when adjusting for inflation), and then jumped to $1.5 billion in FY2007 as DHS created a new Border Security Fencing, Infrastructure, and Technology (BSFIT) account and appropriated money to pay for the border fencing mandate in the Secure Fence Act of 2006. BSFIT appropriations have fallen every year since FY2007, reaching $324 million in FY2013.

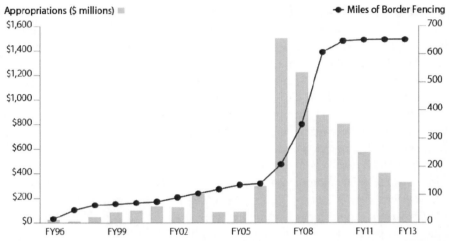

Sources: INS   Congressional   Budget   Justifications   FY2001-FY2003;   DHS
       Congressional Budget Justifications FY2005-2007; DHS Appropriations bills
       FY2007-FY2013.
Notes: In FY2003, immigration inspections from the former INS, customs inspections
       from the former U.S. Customs Service, and USBP were merged to form the
       Bureau of Customs and Border Protection within DHS. As a result, data for years
       prior to FY2003 may not be comparable with the data for FY2004 and after. Data
       for FY1996-FY2002 include USBP construction and tactical infrastructure
       accounts. Construction account funding has been used to fund a number of
       projects at the border, including fencing, vehicle barriers, roads, and USBP
       stations and checkpoints. Funding for FY1998-FY2000 includes San Diego
       fencing as well as fencing, light, and road projects in El Centro, Tucson, El Paso,
       and Marfa. Data for FY2003-FY2006 include DHS construction and tactical
       appropriations. Data for FY2007-FY2012 include total appropriations to CBP's
       Border Security Fencing, Infrastructure, and Technology (BSFIT) account. This
       account funds the construction of fencing, other infrastructure such as roads and
       vehicle barriers, as well as border technologies such as cameras and sensors.

Figure 4. Tactical Infrastructure Appropriations and Miles of Border Fencing, FY1996-FY2012.

Surveillance Assets

The Border Patrol uses advanced technology to augment its agents' ability to patrol the border. USBP's border surveillance system has its origins in the former Immigration and Naturalization Service's (INS's) Integrated Surveillance Information System (ISIS), initiated in 1998. ISIS was folded into a broader border surveillance system named the America's Shield Initiative (ASI) in 2005, and ASI was made part of DHS' Secure Border Initiative (SBI) the following year, with the surveillance program renamed SBI*net* and managed under contract by the Boeing Corporation.

Under all three of these names, the system consisted of a network of remote video surveillance (RVS) systems (including cameras and infrared systems), and sensors (including seismic, magnetic, and thermal detectors), linked into a computer network, known as the Integrated Computer Assisted Detection (ICAD) database. The system was intended to ensure seamless coverage of the border by combining the feeds from multiple cameras and sensors into one remote-controlled system linked to a central communications control room at a USBP station or sector headquarters. USBP personnel monitoring the control room screened the ICAD system to re-position RVS cameras toward the location where sensor alarms were tripped. Control room personnel then alerted field agents to the intrusion and coordinated the response.

All three of these systems struggled to meet deployment timelines and to provide USBP with the promised level of border surveillance.[74] DHS also faced criticism of ASI and SBI*net* for noncompetitive contracting practices, inadequate oversight of contractors, and cost overruns.[75] DHS Secretary Napolitano ordered a department-wide assessment of the SBI*net* technology project in January 2010 and suspended the SBI*net* contract in March 2010.[76] The review confirmed SBI*net*'s history of "continued and repeated technical problems, cost overruns, and schedule delays, raising serious questions about the system's ability to meet the needs for technology along the border."[77] DHS terminated SBI*net* in January 2011.

Under the department's current Arizona Surveillance Technology Plan, the Border Patrol deploys a mix of different surveillance technologies designed to meet the specific needs of different border regions. As of November 2012, deployed assets included 337 Remote Video Surveillance Systems (RVSS) consisting of fixed daylight and infrared cameras that transmit images to a central location (up from 269 in 2006), 198 short and medium range Mobile Vehicle Surveillance Systems (MVSS) mounted on trucks and monitored in the truck's passenger compartment (up from zero in 2005) and 41 long range Mobile Surveillance Systems (MSS, up from zero in 2005), 12 hand-held agent portable medium range surveillance systems (APSS, up from zero in 2005), 15 Integrated Fixed Towers that were developed as part of the SBInet system (up from zero in 2005), and 13,406 unattended ground sensors (up from about 11,200 in 2005).[78] According to CBP officials, the department's acquisitions strategy now emphasizes flexible equipment and mobile technology that permits USBP to surge surveillance capacity in a particular region, and off-the-shelf technology in order to hold down costs and get resources on the ground more quickly. Rather than run surveillance monitoring through a station or sector dispatcher, the agency is also experimenting with "real time" dispatching that allows agents in the field to monitor surveillance equipment directly. [79]

Aerial and Marine Surveillance

In addition to these ground-based surveillance assets, CBP deploys manned and unmanned aircraft as well as marine vessels to conduct surveillance. Air and marine vessels patrol regions of the border that are inaccessible to other surveillance assets, with unmanned aerial systems (UAS) deployed in areas considered too high-risk for manned aircraft or personnel on the ground.[80] In FY2012, CBP's Office of Air and Marine deployed 19 types of aircraft and three classes of marine vessels, for a total of 269 aircraft and 293 marine vessels operating from over 70 locations.[81] The agency reported 81,045 flight hours (down from about 95,000 in FY2011) and 47,742 underway hours in marine vessels (down from about 133,000 in FY2011).[82] As of November 2012, CBP operated a total of 10 UAS up from zero in 2006, including 2 UAS on the Northern border, 5 on the Southwest border, and 3 in the Gulf of Mexico.[83] UAS accounted for 5,737 flight hours in FY2012, up from 4,406 hours in FY2011.[84]

With support from Department of Defense (DOD), CBP conducted an evaluation of two unmanned aerostat (tethered blimp) systems during the summer of 2012: the Persistent Ground Surveillance System (PGSS) and the Rapid Aerostat Initial Deployment (RAID). In addition, CBP evaluated PGSS and RAID towers, which support aerostat deployment as well as ground-based technologies. These two systems have been deployed by the military to conduct area surveillance. As a result of the evaluation, CBP concluded that these systems could provide useful support to CBP operations on the border; and CBP reportedly is working with DOD to identify opportunities to transfer ownership of aerostats returning from overseas to CBP.[85]

BORDER PATROL ENFORCEMENT DATA

For 90 years, the Border Patrol has recorded the number of deportable aliens apprehended in the United States;[86] and alien apprehensions remain the agency's primary indicator of immigration enforcement. The agency also collects several additional measures of immigration enforcement, including unique apprehensions, alien recidivism, and estimated turn backs and got aways. These enforcement outcomes provide insight into the state of the border, as discussed in this section, but they confront certain limitations when it comes to estimating illegal border inflows (see **"Metrics for Evaluating Border Security"**).

Alien Apprehensions

Figure 5 depicts total USBP apprehensions of deportable and removable aliens for FY1960- FY2012. Apprehensions are widely understood to be correlated with illegal flows, and the data in Figure 5 reflect historical trends in unauthorized migration (see "Border Patrol History and Strategy"). Thus, apprehensions were very low in the 1960s, but climbed sharply in the two decades after 1965. Apprehensions reached an all-time high of 1.7 million in 1986 and again in 2000, and an average of more than 1.2 million apprehensions per year were recorded 1983-2006, reflecting high levels of unauthorized migration throughout this period. As Figure 5 also illustrates, apprehensions have fallen sharply since 2000, and particularly since 2006. The 340,252 apprehensions observed in 2011 were the lowest level since 1971, and the 364,768 apprehensions in 2012 were the second-lowest level since that time. Falling apprehensions likely reflect fewer illegal inflows since 2006, though the degree to which reduced inflows are a result of effective enforcement versus other factors like the recent U.S. economic downturn remains subject to debate (see "How Secure is the U.S. Border?").

Southwest Border Apprehensions by Sector
Figure 6 depicts apprehensions along the Southwest border for FY1992- FY2012, broken down by certain Border Patrol sectors. The sector-specific apprehension pattern generally adheres to the predictions of the 1994 National Strategic Plan. Increased enforcement in the El Paso and San Diego sectors was associated with high apprehensions in those sectors during the early 1990s, and then with falling apprehensions by the middle of the decade.

Apprehensions in the San Diego and El Paso sectors remained well below their early-1990s levels throughout the following decade— findings that suggest border enforcement in those sectors has been broadly effective.

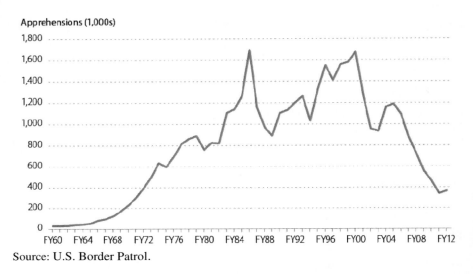

Source: U.S. Border Patrol.

Figure 5. Total USBP Apprehensions of Deportable Aliens, FY1960-FY2012.

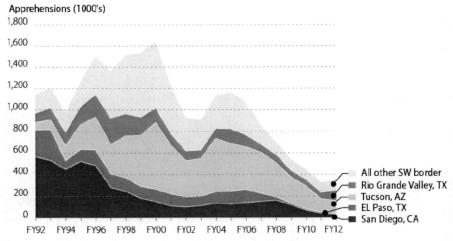

Source: USBP, Total Apprehensions by Southwest Border Sectors.

Figure 6. U.S. Border Patrol Apprehensions of Deportable Aliens, Southwest Border, by Selected Sectors, FY1992-FY2012.

Falling apprehensions in San Diego and El Paso during the late 1990s initially were more than offset by rising apprehensions in the Tucson, AZ sector and other border locations, including the Laredo and Del Rio, TX sectors. Since FY2011, apprehensions in Tucson have fallen back to their lowest level since 1993, but apprehensions in the Rio Grande Valley have increased, and now account for more than a quarter of Southwest border apprehensions.[87] Thus, since the initiation of the prevention through deterrence approach in the mid-1990s, it appears that success in San Diego and El Paso may have come at the expense of Tucson and other sectors; and recent enforcement in Arizona may be pushing some unauthorized flows into South Texas.

Unique Subjects and Alien Recidivism

Overall apprehensions data record apprehension *events*, and therefore count certain individuals more than once because they enter and are apprehended multiple times. Since 2000, the Border Patrol also has tracked the number of *unique subjects* the agency apprehends per year by analyzing biometric data (i.e., fingerprints and digital photographs) of persons apprehended.[88] As **Figure 7** illustrates, trends in unique subjects apprehended are similar to total apprehensions: falling from 2000-2003, climbing in 2004-2005, and then falling sharply from about 818,000 in 2005 to about 247,000 individuals in 2011, before climbing back to 284,000 in FY2012.

Significantly, the gap between total and unique apprehensions has steadily narrowed, with unique subjects representing 54-55% of total apprehensions in 2000-2001, 65-70% in 2002-2010, and 75-80% in 2011-2012. Put another way, each unique subject is being apprehended fewer times, on average, with the aggregate average number of apprehensions per person apprehended (i.e., total apprehensions divided by unique subjects) falling from 1.9 apprehensions per person in 2000 to 1.3 apprehensions per person in 2012.[89]

This trend is explained, in part, by the bars in **Figure 7**, which depict annual Southwest border recidivism rates, which USBP has tracked since 2005. The Border Patrol defines the annual recidivism rate as the percentage of unique subjects apprehended more than once in a given fiscal year. A goal of the Consequence Delivery System has been to deter aliens from re-entering—i.e., to reduce recidivism. As **Figure 7** illustrates, recidivism rates increased slightly between 2005 (25%) and 2007 (29%), but have fallen since that time, reaching 17% in 2012.

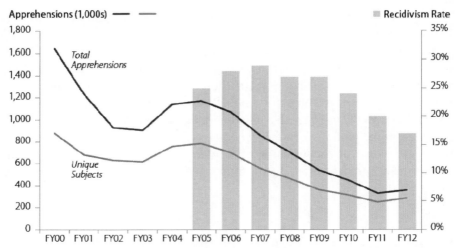

Source: CRS presentation of data provided by CBP Office of Congressional Affairs, March 10, 2013.

Notes: Total apprehensions refer to the total number of USBP apprehensions in Southwest border sectors; u*nique subjects* refers to the number of different people apprehended based on biometric records. The recidivism rate is the percentage of unique individuals apprehended two or more times in a given fiscal year.

Figure 7. USBP Southwest Border Unique Subjects and Recidivism Rates; FY2000-FY2012.

Estimated "Got Aways" and "Turn Backs"

Border Patrol stations and sectors estimate the number of illegal entrants who successfully travel to the U.S. interior and who USBP ceased pursuing, or "got aways." 90 Stations and sectors also estimate "turn backs," the number of people who illegally cross the border but then cross back to Mexico. USBP uses the sum of got aways, turn backs, and apprehensions to estimate *the total number of known illegal entries* (also see "**Border Patrol Effectiveness Rate**"). The agency has used these data since 2006 to inform tactical decision making and to allocate resources across Southwest border sectors, but the Border Patrol has not published them or viewed them as reliable metrics of border security because of challenges associated with measuring got aways and turn backs across different border sectors.[91]

ADDITIONAL BORDER SECURITY DATA: MIGRANT SURVEYS

Apart from Border Patrol data on enforcement outcomes, a second major source of information about unauthorized migration and border security is survey data based on interviews with migrants and potential migrants. Much of the research on unauthorized migration across the Southwest border focuses on Mexicans because Mexico historically accounts for about 95% of persons apprehended at the Southwest border.[92] An advantage to surveys is that they may collect more information about their subjects than is found in enforcement data. In addition, because surveys are conducted within the U.S. interior as well as in migrant countries of origin (i.e., Mexico), surveys may capture more information about successful illegal inflows and about the deterrent effects of enforcement. In 2011, DHS commissioned a comprehensive study by the National Research Council (NRC) on the use of surveys and related methodologies to estimate the number of illegal U.S.-Mexico border crossings; and the NRC recommended that DHS use survey data along with enforcement data to measure illegal flows and the effectiveness of border enforcement.[93]

Two binational (U.S.-Mexican) surveys may be particularly useful for estimating illegal flows because they have examined migration dynamics in migrant-sending and –receiving communities for a number of years. The surveys are the Mexican Migration Field Research Program (MMFRP) based at the University of California-San Diego (UCSD) and the Mexican Migration Project (MMP) based at Princeton University. These targeted surveys ask a number of questions about U.S. immigration enforcement and how it affects respondents' migration histories and future plans. While analysts must account for the likelihood that unauthorized migrants may be less than forthcoming with interviewers and may be under-represented in certain survey samples, a body of social science research has made use of these data and developed commonly cited methodologies to account for these and other challenges.[94]

Probability of Apprehension

The UCSD and Princeton surveys both include data, based on self-reporting by people who have previously attempted to migrate illegally, on the probability that an alien will be apprehended on any given attempted crossing.

According to the Princeton data, the probability of being apprehended on any given crossing averaged about .37 in the two decades before IRCA's passage, ranging from a low of .31 to a high of .42 during this period. The probability of apprehension was somewhat lower in the decade after IRCA's passage, ranging from .22 to .32 between 1986 and 1995, and averaging .26 for the decade. Between 1996 and 2010, the last year for which sufficient data are available, the apprehension rate returned to an average of .36, with a low of .29 and a high of .50 during these years.[95]

The UCSD data suggest slightly higher apprehension rates, and show broadly similar trends. According to these data, the probability of being apprehended on any given crossing averaged .51 between 1974 and 1983, ranging from .32 to .67 during this period. After peaking at .67 in 1981, the probability of apprehension fell steadily to a low of .34 in 1992-1993. Since 1994 the probability of apprehension has averaged .49, ranging from .30 to .58 during this period.[96] The UCSD and the Princeton estimates of apprehension rates are substantially lower than the Border Patrol's current estimate, which is between .67 and .86.[97]

Border Deterrence

While the Princeton and UCSD surveys thus find that unauthorized migrants are apprehended about a third to one-half of the time on any given crossing attempt, both surveys find that most aliens who attempt to cross illegally eventually succeed, meaning border deterrence rates are low. According to the Princeton data, between 75% and 90% of aliens apprehended at the border between 1965 and 2009 made a subsequent attempt to re-enter the United States and between 55% and 88% eventually succeeded. Border deterrence (i.e., the proportion of aliens who *failed* to re-enter the United States) averaged 37% in the two decades before IRCA's passage; averaged 26% between 1986 and 1995, reaching an all-time low of 21% in 1989; and averaged 34% in 1996-2009, the last year for which sufficient data are available. The UCSD survey finds at the border deterrence rates below 10% for the entire post-1980 period.[98]

Smuggling Fees

Princeton and UCSD surveys indicate that the majority of unauthorized migrants to the United States make use of human smugglers (often referred to in Mexico as "coyotes" or "polleros") to facilitate their illegal admission to the country. Indeed, whereas about 80% of unauthorized migrants from Mexico reportedly relied on human smugglers during the 1980s, about 90% did so in 2005-2007, though the use of smugglers may have declined a bit during the recent economic downturn.[99] Migrants' reliance on human smugglers, along with prices charged by smugglers, are an additional potential indicator of the effectiveness of U.S. border enforcement efforts, as more effective enforcement should increase the costs to smugglers of bringing migrants across the border, with smugglers passing such costs along to their clients in the form of higher fees.[100]

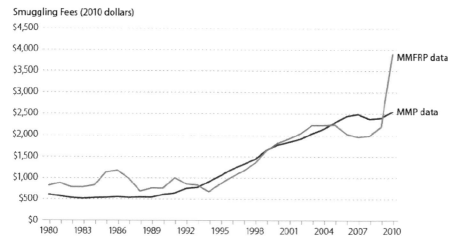

Source: Princeton University Mexican Migration Project (MMP) and University of California, San Diego Mexican Migration Field Research Program (MMFRP).

Notes: Data based on surveys of unauthorized Mexican migrants about their most recent unauthorized trip to the United States, with reported amounts adjusted for inflation using Bureau of Labor Statistics Consumer Price Index Research Series Using Current Methods (CPI-R-US). Data are a weighted three-year average to account for a small sample size. MMFRP estimate for 2010 may be unreliable due to a small sample size for that year.

Figure 8. Smuggling Fees Paid by Unauthorized Mexican Migrants, 1980-2010.

Figure 8 summarizes data from the Princeton and UCSD surveys describing average smuggling fees paid by certain unauthorized migrants from Mexico to the United States. In both cases, the data reflect reported smuggling fees based on surveys conducted with unauthorized migrants in the United States and in Mexico (i.e., after migrants had returned home), with fees adjusted for inflation and reported in 2010 dollars.

According to these data, smuggling fees were mostly flat between 1980 and 1993, at about $600- $850, with an average annual real growth rate of 1.5 – 2.0%. Smuggling fees in both samples began to rise beginning around 1994, and climbed by an average of 11% per year between 1994 and 2002, reaching about $2,000 in both samples by 2002. Growth in smuggling fees has been slower since then, averaging 3.7% per year in the Princeton sample and 1.8% in the UCSD sample (excluding data from 2010, a year in which a small sample may have resulted in an unreliable annual estimate).[101] Thus, these data suggest that crossing the border illegally became somewhat more difficult—or at least most expensive—in the decade after the USBP began to implement its 1994 national strategy.

METRICS OF BORDER SECURITY

Some Members of Congress and others have asked the Border Patrol to provide a clear measure of how many aliens cross the border illegally and/or of the overall state of border security,[102] but measuring illegal border flows is difficult for the obvious reason that unauthorized aliens seek to avoid detection. While the Border Patrol has accurate data on various *enforcement outcomes*, these enforcement data were not designed to measure overall *illegal inflows*. Thus, DHS officials have testified that current enforcement data do not offer a suitable metric to describe border security.[103]

Apprehensions data are imperfect indicators of illegal flows because they exclude two important groups when it comes to unauthorized migration: aliens who successfully enter and remain in the United States (i.e., enforcement failures) and aliens who are deterred from entering the United States (i.e., certain enforcement successes). Thus, analysts do not know if a decline in apprehensions is an indicator of successful enforcement, because fewer people are attempting to enter, or of enforcement failures, because more of them are succeeding.[104] A further limitation to apprehensions data is that they count events, not unique individuals, so the same person may appear multiple times in the dataset after multiple entry attempts.

Unique apprehensions and USBP's estimate of got aways and turn backs are designed, in part, to address these limitations, but they offer only partial solutions. Unique apprehensions address the "overcount" problem associated with recidivism, but still misses information about certain enforcement failures (got-aways) and certain enforcement successes (deterrence). Estimated got aways and turn backs attempt to grapple with the latter problem; but (like apprehensions) they count events rather than individuals. Moreover, because estimated got-aways and turn backs attempt to measure enforcement outcomes that do not result in apprehensions, they are heavily dependent on the subjective judgment of individual border agents.[105] To the extent that agents— or the agency—are rewarded for effective enforcement, some people may question the credibility of a measure based on such judgments. Indeed, some media reports already have raised questions about the accuracy of the got away and turn back data.[106] The Border Patrol issued new guidance in September 2012 designed to impose greater consistency on turn back and got away data collection and reporting,[107] but data from the new system have not yet been analyzed.

A further limitation of enforcement data is that all such data depend on enforcement resources. In general, USBP enforcement outcomes (e.g., apprehensions, estimated got aways) are a function of 1) the underlying illegal flows, and 2) the agency's ability to detect such flows. Enforcement data alone cannot disentangle these two factors. As a result, enforcement data may tend to overestimate illegal flows where resources are robust, and to under-estimate such flows where resources are scarce.

Given the limits of existing border enforcement data, DHS and outside researchers have developed several different metrics for estimating illegal border flows and describing border security. Three different methods for estimating illegal migration stocks and flows are described in the remainder of this section, and broad conclusions based on these metrics are described below (see "How Secure is the U.S. Border?").[108]

The Residual Method for Estimating Unauthorized Residents in the United States

Arguably the most well-developed approach to measuring unauthorized migration focuses on the number of unauthorized migrants residing in the United States. For many years, analysts within DHS and other social scientists have used the so-called "residual method" to estimate this number. In essence, the method involves using legal admissions data to estimate the legal, foreign-born population, and then subtracting this number from the overall count of foreign-born residents based on U.S. census data.[109]

The residual method provides limited information about the border *per se* because many unauthorized residents enter the United States through ports of entry, lawfully or otherwise.[110] Nonetheless, estimates of the size of the unauthorized population may offer several advantages over the border metrics discussed below. First, for many people, how many unauthorized aliens reside within the United States ultimately is a more important question than how many cross the border. After all, if illegal border flows fall to zero, but many people continue to enter illegally through ports of entry or by overstaying nonimmigrant visas, many people would consider such an outcome problematic. Second, for this reason, the size of the unauthorized population more comprehensively reflects how well immigration policy and immigration enforcement function, including for example the effectiveness of worksite and other interior enforcement as well as how well visas meet employer and family demands. Third, estimates of the unauthorized population offer the advantage of a nearly 30-year track record and a relatively uncontroversial methodology. As long ago as 2001, the Department of Justice used the total estimated stock of unauthorized migrants in the United States as a key performance metric for the department's evaluation of its border security efforts.[111]

CBP Metrics of Border Security

Operational Control of the Border

Section 2 of the Secure Fence Act of 2006 (P.L. 109-367) defines operational control of the border to mean "the prevention of all unlawful entries into the United States, including entries by terrorists, other unlawful aliens, instruments of terrorism, narcotics, and other contraband." Most experts agree that preventing 100% of unlawful entries across U.S. borders is an impossible task;[112] and through FY2010, the Border Patrol classified portions of the border as being under "effective" or "operational" control if the agency "has the ability to detect, respond, and interdict illegal activity at the border or after entry into the United States."[113] The agency conducted a five-level assessment of border security, with the two top levels ("controlled" and "managed") defined as being under effective control, and the three remaining levels ("monitored," "low-level monitored," and "remote/low activity") defined as not being under effective control.[114] In February 2010, the Border

Patrol reported that 1,107 miles (57%) of the Southwest border were under effective control.[115]

Beginning in FY2011, USBP stopped using this measure of effective control.[116] The agency reportedly no longer views operational or effective control as a useful metric because station and sector chiefs could not accurately and reliably use the five-level coding scheme to assess different border regions.[117] In addition, given the dynamic nature of border threats, the agency does not view it as useful to evaluate border security on a mile-by-mile basis.[118]

Border Conditions Index

In May 2011, DHS announced that CBP was developing a new "border conditions index" (BCI).[119] Reportedly, the BCI will include measures of estimated illegal flows between ports of entry, wait times and the efficiency of legal flows at ports of entry, and public safety and quality of life in border regions. These three components will be combined to develop a holistic "score" calculated for different regions of the border.[120] With these different components, the BCI includes some of the same information some Members of Congress and others may consider to be of interest with respect to describing border security; but DHS officials have emphasized that the BCI encompasses a broader set of issues than "border security" as this term is normally used, and that the BCI therefore may not satisfy demands for a single comprehensive measure of border security.[121] Officials have also testified that the BCI remains in the development phase.[122]

Border Patrol Effectiveness Rate

By dividing apprehensions and estimated turn backs (i.e., successful enforcement outcomes) by estimated known illegal entries (see "**Estimated 'Got Aways' and 'Turn Backs'**"), USBP calculates an *estimated enforcement effectiveness rate*. Some people have proposed using this effectiveness rate as a measure of border security. While using enforcement data to measure border security raises a number of methodological concerns (see "**Metrics of Border Security**"), the effectiveness *rate* would have an advantage over other enforcement metrics because, as a ratio, it may be somewhat less sensitive to the level of enforcement resources in place.[123] As with the BCI, it is difficult to evaluate USBP's effectiveness rate as a border metric because little is known about the agency's new protocols for collecting got away and turn back data.

Estimating Illegal Flows Using Recidivism Data

For many years, social scientists have used the so-called "capture-recapture" method to estimate unauthorized flows based on recidivism data.[124] The capture-recapture method estimates the total flow of unauthorized migrants based on the ratio of persons re-apprehended after an initial enforcement action to the total number of persons apprehended.[125] In the basic model, the probability of apprehension is calculated by taking the ratio of recidivist apprehensions to total apprehensions; and the total illegal inflow is calculated by dividing total apprehensions by the odds of apprehension.[126] See **Appendix A** for more details.

An advantage to the capture-recapture method is that it relies on observable administrative enforcement data—apprehensions and recidivists—to calculate key border security metrics: apprehension rates and illegal flows. Yet the basic model assumes that all intending unauthorized migrants eventually succeed (i.e., that none are deterred at the border).[127] To the extent that the build-up in border enforcement resources and the deployment of the Consequence Delivery System cause some would-be unauthorized migrants to give up and return home, the capture-recapture method *underestimates* successful enforcement and *overestimates* illegal flows. Likewise, the basic model assumes that all border crossers originate in—and are repatriated to—Mexico, facilitating re-entry attempts. As the proportion of border crossers from countries other than Mexico increases—as it has in recent years—[128] repatriated aliens may be less likely to attempt re-entry, an additional reason the capture-recapture model may over-estimate illegal inflows.

Thus, to estimate illegal flows based on the capture-recapture method, enforcement data on apprehensions and repeat apprehensions must be supplemented with additional information about the proportion of migrants deterred, and must control for lower recidivism rates among nonMexicans.[129] Estimates of illegal flows based on this methodology are discussed below (see **"How Secure is the U.S. Border?"**).

HOW SECURE IS THE U.S. BORDER?

While no single metric accurately and reliably describes border security (see **"Metrics of Border Security"**), most analysts agree, based on available data, that the number of illegal border crossers fell sharply between about 2005 and 2011, with some rise in illegal flows in 2012. This conclusion is supported by key Border Patrol enforcement data described above, including the drop in total apprehensions, the drop in unique apprehensions, and the drop in estimated got aways and total estimated known entries across eight out of nine Border Patrol sectors.

Survey data confirm an apparent drop in illegal inflows, and measure such effects away from the border. For example, according to data collected by the Princeton Mexican Migration Project, an average of about 2% of all Mexican men initiated a first unauthorized trip to the United States each year between 1973 and 2002; but that percentage has fallen sharply since 2002, to below 0.4% in 2008-2011.[130] Estimates of the unauthorized population based on the residual method report drops of about one million unauthorized migrants living in the United States, from about 12.4 million in 2007 to 11.1 million in 2011.[131] And the Pew Hispanic Center estimates that net (i.e., northbound minus southbound) unauthorized migration from Mexico fell to about zero in 2011, and that outflows may have even exceeded inflows.[132]

According to GAO's analysis of Border Patrol metrics, eight out of nine Border Patrol sectors (all except the Big Bend sector) showed improved effectiveness rates between FY2006 and FY2011.[133] In the Tucson sector, the main focus of GAO's analysis, the effectiveness rate improved from 67 to 87 percent during this period. The San Diego, El Centro, Yuma, and El Paso sectors all had effectiveness rates in FY2011 of about 90%; the Del Rio and Laredo sectors (along with Tucson) had rates above 80%; and the Big Bend and Rio Grande Valley sectors had rates between 60 and 70%.

CRS estimates based on USBP recidivism data and using the capture-recapture method also suggest that illegal flows between ports of entry fell substantially between 2005 and 2011, before rising somewhat in 2012 (see **Figure 9**). The shaded area in **Figure 9** depicts total estimated illegal inflows, which are equal to the total number of apprehensions divided by the estimated odds of successful enforcement. (See **Appendix A** for a discussion of the methodology used to generate **Figure 9**.) Based on available data, the figure assumes deterrence rates in 2000-2012 were between 20% (the estimates depicted by the upper bound of the shaded area) and 40% (the lower bound). As the figure indicates, total estimated illegal inflows fell from a high of between 760,000 and 1.4 million in 2004 to a low of between 340,000 and 580,000 in 2009-2010.[134] The model estimates that total illegal inflows were between 400,000 and 660,000 in 2012. Although recidivism data are not available to make similar calculations for previous years, apprehension levels and survey data from the 1980s and 1990s suggest that total illegal inflows likely were lower in 2007-2012 that an any other point in the last three decades.

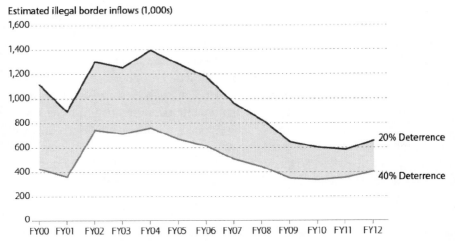

Source: CRS Analysis based on data provided by CBP Office of Congressional
     Affairs.
Notes: See text for discussion of methodology.

Figure 9. Total Estimated Illegal Border Inflows, by Assumed Rate of Deterrence;
FY2000-FY2012.

Border enforcement is only one of several factors that affect illegal
migration.[135] Thus, if illegal entries indeed fell after 2006, to what degree is
this change attributable to enforcement versus other developments, such as the
U.S. economic downturn since 2007, and/or economic and demographic
changes in Mexico and other countries of origin?[136] Disentangling the effects
of enforcement from other factors influencing migration flows is particularly
difficult in the current case because many of the most significant new
enforcement efforts—including a sizeable share of new border enforcement
personnel, most border fencing, new enforcement practices at the border, and
many of the new migration enforcement measures within the United States—
all have occurred at the same time as the most severe recession since the
1930s.

Nonetheless, the drop in recidivism rates suggests that an increasing
proportion of aliens are being deterred by CBP's enforcement efforts, a finding
that also appears to be reflected in survey data from the Princeton survey (see
"Border Deterrence"). Surveys of unauthorized migrants repatriated to

Mexico in 2005 and 2010 also suggest that enforcement is increasingly likely to deter future immigration.[137] As **Figure 9** illustrates, the more unauthorized migrants are being deterred by U.S. enforcement efforts, the lower is the number of successful illegal inflows implied by current enforcement data.

Academic research from 2012 also provides evidence that border enforcement has contributed to a reduction in illegal flows.[138] These findings are noteworthy, in part, because they contradict earlier academic research, much of which found that border enforcement had a limited impact or even was counter-productive when it came to migration control efforts (also see **"Migration Flows: Caging Effects and Alternative Modes of Entry"**).[139] This research suggests that the recent build-up in immigration enforcement at the border and within the United States may have had a greater deterrent effect on illegal migration than earlier efforts.[140] Nonetheless, some uncertainty will remain about the true level of border security as long as U.S. employment demand remains below historic levels.

UNINTENDED AND SECONDARY CONSEQUENCES OF BORDER ENFORCEMENT

The preceding discussion includes estimates of what may be described as the primary costs and benefits of border enforcement, defined in terms of congressional appropriations and deployment of enforcement resources on one hand, and alien apprehensions and other indicators of successful enforcement on the other. A comprehensive analysis of the costs and benefits of border enforcement policies may also consider possible unintended and secondary consequences. Such consequences may produce both costs and benefits—many of which are difficult to measure—in at least five areas: border-area crime and migrant deaths, migrant flows, environmental impacts, effects on border communities, and U.S. foreign relations.

Border-Area Crime and Migrant Deaths

Illegal border crossing is associated with a certain level of border crime and violence and, in the most unfortunate cases, with deaths of illegal border crossers and border-area law enforcement officers. Unauthorized migration may be associated with crime and mortality in at least three distinct ways.

First, unauthorized migration is associated with crime—apart from the crime of illegal entry—because some unauthorized migrants contract with immigrant smugglers and because unauthorized migrants may engage in related illegal activity, such as document fraud. Yet fear of the police may make unauthorized aliens *less* likely to engage in other types of criminal activity, and research on the subject finds low immigrant criminality rates, especially when accounting for education levels and other demographic characteristics.[141] Second, unauthorized migrants may also be likely to be targeted and become crime victims, including victims of violent crime, because they may carry large amounts of cash and may be reluctant to interact with law enforcement officials.[142] Third, illegal border crossers face risks associated with crossing the border at dangerous locations, where they may die from exposure or from drowning.[143]

Border *enforcement* therefore may affect crime and migrant mortality in complex ways.[144] On one hand, the concentration of enforcement resources around the border may exacerbate adverse outcomes by making migrants more likely to rely on smugglers, as noted above (see "**Smuggling Fees**"). The 1994 National Strategic Plan *predicted* a short-term rise in border violence for these reasons.[145] On the other hand, to the extent that enforcement successfully deters illegal crossers, such prevention should reduce crime and mortality. The concentration of law enforcement personnel near the border may further enhance public safety and migrant protection, especially where CBP has made a priority of protecting vulnerable populations.[146]

The empirical record suggests that there is *no significant difference* in the average violent crime rate in border and non-border metropolitan areas.[147] Indeed, the border cities El Paso, TX and San Diego, CA are regularly listed among the safest large cities in the country based on their rankings among similarly sized cities in the Federal Bureau of Investigation's Uniform Crime Report.[148] The specific impact of border enforcement on border-area crime is unknown, however, because available data cannot separate the influence of border enforcement from other factors.[149]

With respect to mortality, available data about migrant deaths along the Southwest border are presented in **Figure 10**. The figures come from academic research based on local medical investigators' and examiners' offices in California, Arizona, New Mexico, and Texas between 1985 and 1998 (the University of Houston's Center for Immigration Research, CIR); Mexican foreign ministry and Mexican media counts compiled by the American Civil Liberties Union of San Diego; and data compiled by DHS based on bodies recovered on the U.S. side of the border.[150] All three data sources reflect *known* migrant deaths, and therefore undercount actual migrant deaths since some bodies may not be discovered.[151] Additionally, U.S. data sources generally do not include information from the Mexican side of the border and therefore further undercount migration-related fatalities.

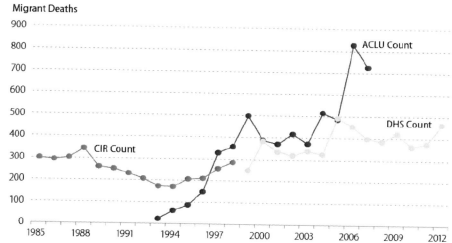

Source: University of Houston Center for Immigration Research (CIR); Jimenez, "Humanitarian Crisis," 2009 (ACLU); CBP Office of Congressional Affairs March 13, 2013 (DHS).

Figure 10. Known Migrant Deaths, Southwest Border, 1985-2012.

As **Figure 10** illustrates, data from the CIR indicate that known migrant deaths fell from a high of 344 in 1988 to a low of 171 in 1994 before climbing back to 286 in 1998. According to DHS data, known migrant deaths climbed from 250 in 1999 to 492 in 2005, and averaged 431 deaths per year in 2005-2009. DHS's count fell to an average of 369 per year in 2010-2011, but increased to 463 in FY2012. And the ACLU found that known migrant deaths increased from just 80 per year in 1993-1996 to 496 per year in 1997-2007. The apparent increase in migrant deaths is noteworthy in light of the apparent decline in unauthorized entries during the same period. These data offer evidence that border crossings have become more hazardous since the "prevention through deterrence" policy went into effect in the 1990s,[152] though (as with crime) the precise impact of enforcement on migrant deaths is unknown.

Migration Flows: "Caging" Effects and Alternative Modes of Entry

With illegal border crossing becoming more dangerous and more expensive, some unauthorized aliens appear to have adapted their behavior to avoid crossing the border via traditional pathways. Most notably, social science research suggests that border enforcement has had the unintended consequence of encouraging unauthorized aliens to settle permanently in the United States rather than working temporarily and then returning home, as was more common prior to the mid-1980s.[153] The primary evidence for this so-called "caging" effect is that unauthorized migrants appear to be staying longer in the United States and raising families here more often rather than making regular trips to visit families that remain in countries of origin.[154] Although other factors also likely contribute to these changes,[155] survey results appear to confirm that border enforcement has been a factor behind these longer stays.[156]

A second unintended consequence of enhanced border enforcement between ports of entry may have been an increase in illegal entries through ports of entry and other means. According to UCSD Mexico Migration Field Research Program research, unauthorized Mexican migrants from one community in Mexico interviewed in 2009 used six different methods to enter the United States illegally, with one in four such aliens passing illegally through a port of entry by using borrowed or fraudulent documents or by hiding in a vehicle.[157] Based on three different surveys conducted between 2008 and 2010, UCSD researchers found that the probability of being apprehended while passing illegally though a port of entry was about half as high as the probability of being apprehended while crossing between the ports.[158] CBP's Passenger Compliance Examination (COMPEX) System reportedly detects very little illegal migration through ports of entry, however.[159] There is also anecdotal evidence that unauthorized aliens have recently turned to maritime routes as alternative strategies to cross the U.S.-Mexican border.[160]

Environmental Impact

A third set of potential unintended consequences concern the effect of border enforcement on the environment. As with the effects of enforcement on border crime and violence, the effects of enforcement on the environment are complex because they reflect changes in migrant behavior and the secondary effects of enforcement per se.

On one hand, many illegal border crossers transit through sensitive environmental areas, cutting vegetation for shelter and fire, potentially causing wildfires, increasing erosion through repeated use of trails, and discarding trash.[161] Thus, to the extent that border enforcement successfully deters illegal flows, enforcement benefits the environment by reducing these undesirable outcomes. On the other hand, the construction of fencing, roads, and other tactical infrastructure may damage border-area ecosystems. These environmental considerations may be especially important because much of the border runs through remote and environmentally sensitive areas.[162] For this reason, even when accounting for the possible environmental benefits of reduced illegal border flows, some environmental groups have opposed border infrastructure projects because they threaten rare and endangered species as well as other wildlife by damaging ecosystems and restricting the movement of animals, and because surveillance towers and artificial night lighting have detrimental effects on migrant birds.[163]

Effects on Border Communities and Civil Rights

Although economists disagree about the overall economic impact of unauthorized migration, unauthorized migrants may impose a number of costs at the local level, including through their use of schools and other public programs.[164] Some are also concerned that illegal migration undermines the rule of law. For these reasons, successful border enforcement may benefit border communities by reducing illegal inflows.

Yet some business owners on the Southwest and Northern borders have complained that certain border enforcement efforts threaten their economic activities, including farming and ranching activities that are disrupted by the deployment of USBP resources to the border and commercial activities that suffer from reduced regional economic activity.[165] More generally, some people have complained that the construction of barriers divides communities that have straddled international land borders for generations.[166]

Some people have raised additional concerns about the effects of border enforcement on civil rights. Some residents of Southwest and Northern border communities see enhanced border enforcement as leading to racial profiling and wrongful detentions.[167] On top of this general concern, some people argue that Operation Streamline raises additional questions about whether migrants receive adequate legal protections during fast-tracked criminal procedures.[168] And some have argued that mistreatment and abuse are widespread in CBP detention facilities.[169]

An additional concern that some have raised about CBP's focus on high consequence enforcement is the possibility that focusing scarce judicial and prosecutorial resources on immigration enforcement diverts attention from more serious crimes.[170] A 2013 Justice Department study found that the number of immigration defendants in federal courts increased 664% between 1995 and 2010 (from 5,103 to 39,001); and that immigration cases accounted for 60% of the overall increase in pretrial detentions during that period.[171] More generally, immigration offenders accounted for 46% of federal arrests in 2010, outnumbering all other crimes and up from 22% a decade earlier.[172] A 2008 study by the Administrative Office of the U.S. Courts found that while Congress had provided short-term funding to allow the courts to respond to increased prosecutions, the courts faced a shortage of suitable courthouse and detention facilities in some border locations.[173]

Effects on Regional Relations

What are the effects of U.S. border enforcement policies on U.S. relations with its continental neighbors, Mexico and Canada? The United States and Canada have a strong record of collaborative border enforcement, including through 15 binational, multi-agency Integrated Border Enforcement Teams (IBETs) operating at 24 locations at and between U.S.-Canadian ports of entry. In February 2011, President Obama and Prime Minister Harper signed the Beyond the Border declaration, which described their shared visions for a common approach to perimeter security and economic competitiveness; and the countries released an Action Plan on December 7, 2011, to implement the agreement.[174] While some Canadians have raised objections to some of the information sharing and joint law enforcement provisions of the agreement,[175] border enforcement between the ports has not been identified as a significant source of bilateral tension.

The United States and Mexico also cooperate extensively on border enforcement operations at the Southwest border.[176] Yet immigration enforcement occasionally has been a source of bilateral tension. And with Mexicans being the most frequent target of U.S. immigration enforcement efforts, some Mexicans have expressed concerns about the construction of border fencing, the effects of border enforcement on migrant deaths, and the protection of unaccompanied minors and other vulnerable groups, among other issues related to immigration enforcement.[177]

Conclusion: Understanding the Costs and Benefits of Border Enforcement between Ports of Entry

The United States has focused substantial resources along its land borders to prevent and control illegal migration since the 1980s, with investments in personnel, fencing, and surveillance assets all up significantly in the post 9/11 period, in particular. Since 2005, CBP also has transformed its approach to managing enforcement outcomes, through its Consequence Delivery System.

Measuring the *effects* of border enforcement is difficult. On one hand, after reaching a high point in 2000, Border Patrol apprehensions fell sharply in 2007-2011, reaching a 42-year low in FY2011. The Border Patrol's IDENT database also indicates a declining proportion of aliens is apprehended more than once (i.e., recidivism is down). Estimates based on enforcement and survey data and accounting for estimated apprehension and deterrence rates suggest that total illegal inflows in 2009-2011 were well below levels observed in the two decades after IRCA's passage, but that illegal inflows increased somewhat in 2012.

On the other hand, there is also some evidence that migrants have adapted to more difficult conditions at the border by using other means to enter the United States and by remaining longer. A comprehensive accounting also may consider various potential unintended consequences of border enforcement on the civil rights of legal residents and U.S. citizens in the border region, on migrants' human rights, on the quality of life in border communities, on the environment and wildlife, and on U.S.-regional relations.

What do these findings mean for Members of Congress who oversee border security and immigration policy? Especially in light of current fiscal constraints, some Members of Congress may evaluate future border enforcement in terms of expected returns on America's investments, and they may consider the possibility that certain additional investments at the border may be met with diminishing returns. Border infrastructure may offer an example: with 651 miles of fencing and barriers already in place along the Southwest border, each additional mile would be in ever more remote locations, and therefore more expensive to install and maintain and likely to deter fewer unauthorized migrants. Similarly, some Members of Congress may question the concrete benefits of deploying more sophisticated surveillance systems across the entire northern and southern borders, including vast regions in which too few personnel are deployed to respond to the occasional illegal entry that may be detected.

Deciding how to allocate border resources therefore requires a clear definition of the goals of border security. Zero admissions of unauthorized migrants may not be a realistic goal when it comes to migration control, as noted above, and is a higher standard than is expected of most law enforcement agencies. While this report focuses on migration control at U.S. borders, border security also encompasses the detection and interdiction of weapons of mass destruction (WMD), narcotics, and other illicit goods; policies to combat human trafficking; and other security goals. These diverse goals are often conflated in an undifferentiated debate about "border security"; but each of these goals may suggest a different mix of border investments, as well as different metrics and different standards for successful enforcement outcomes. Should policies to prevent unauthorized migration be held to the same standards as policies to prevent the entry of WMDs, for example?

Regardless of how these questions are answered in principle, debates about immigration control and border security may benefit from better metrics of border security and illegal migration, and from a more analytical approach to program design. The Border Patrol has taken a step in this direction by analyzing recidivism data as a function of different enforcement outcomes through its Consequence Delivery System. This report also identifies several metrics for measuring border security, all of which have advantages and disadvantages. In the context of immigration policy and a possible immigration reform bill, Members of Congress may choose to focus on the total number of unauthorized aliens in the United States, in addition to border flows, since border enforcement is just one of many factors (along with interior enforcement, visa policies, etc.) influencing the size of the unauthorized population, and because more is known about the population number than about border flows.

APPENDIX A: CAPTURE-RECAPTURE METHODOLOGY

The capture-recapture methodology for estimating unauthorized migration flows based on total and recidivist alien apprehensions was first proposed by the sociologist Thomas Espenshade in 1995.[178] Espenshade's original model assumed that all intending migrants (i.e., everyone who makes an initial crossing attempt) eventually succeed—an assumption supported by academic research at the time.[179] Likewise, the model focused exclusively on unauthorized Mexican migrants, a population of particular interest since Mexicans represented 96% of all alien apprehensions during the 1990s,[180] and since Mexico's long shared border with the United States creates unique enforcement dynamics, including high recidivism rates.

The basic capture-recapture model works backwards from the total number of apprehensions and recidivist apprehensions to calculate total illegal flow and the odds of apprehension. First, by definition, the number of apprehensions is related to the total number of illegal crossings multiplied by the probability of being apprehended on any given attempt. For example, if 1,000 aliens attempt to cross, and the probability of being apprehended on a given trip is 50%, then the number of apprehensions would be 500. If unsuccessful migrants always make a second (and subsequent) attempt to enter, the number of aliens making a second attempt is equal to number of initial apprehensions (i.e., 500 in the previous example); and the number of apprehensions among one-time repeat crossers would be 250. In the following period, 250 would attempt entry and 125 would succeed, and so on. By adding up these iterations, Espenshade shows that the total number of apprehensions (A) is equal to the total flow of unauthorized aliens (F) times the odds of apprehension, where odds are defined statistically as the probability of apprehension (P) divided by one minus the probability of apprehension.[181] Re-arranging this statement to solve for flow:

$$F = A/[P/(1-P)] \qquad (1)$$

Second, the ratio of repeat apprehensions to total apprehensions is used to calculate the probability of apprehension on a given attempt. In short, the formula for repeat apprehensions is simply the formula for total apprehensions times the probability of being apprehended. As a result, repeat apprehensions (R) divided by total apprehensions (A) yields the probability of apprehension ($P_{apprenehsion}$) on a given trip:[182]

$$P_{apprenehsion} = R/A \qquad (2)$$

The methodology used in this report adapts Espenshade's model to account for the fact that some aliens do not make a second or subsequent attempt after being apprehended—i.e., that some are deterred.[183] This modified capture-recapture model also has been used in a 2013 Council on Foreign Relations report;[184] and DHS officials have indicated that DHS's Border Conditions Index, now under development, employs a similar method to estimate illegal flows between ports of entry.[185] In the modified model, the estimated probability of apprehension defined in equation (2) is divided by one minus the probability of deterrence to calculate the probability of successful enforcement ($P_{enforcement}$):

$$P_{enforcement} = (R/A)/(1\text{-}D) \tag{3}$$

Figure 9 in this report was generated by using equation (3) to estimate the probability of successful enforcement at the Southwest border and equation (1) to estimate total Southwest border illegal flows. In the absence of country-specific recidivism rates (and in light of the higher costs to reentry following deportation of non-Mexicans), CRS's analysis assumes non-Mexicans do not re-enter in the same fiscal year. Thus, the calculations for equation (3) use CBP data on total recidivists divided by CBP data on Mexican apprehensions to calculate a Mexico-specific apprehension rate.[186] Based on available survey and USBP turn back data, deterrence rates were assumed to fall between 20 and 40%. CRS further assumed that Mexican and non-Mexican aliens are apprehended at the same rate, and thus uses the value of P calculated in equation (3), along with CBP data on total Southwest border apprehensions, to estimate total Southwest border illegal inflows based on equation (1).

End Notes

[1] The Bracero program was a formal guest worker program managed jointly by the United States and Mexico that admitted about 4.6 million workers between 1942 and 1964.

[2] The estimated population of unauthorized aliens was about 1.7 million by 1979 and about 3.2 million in 1986; most researchers consider earlier estimates of the unauthorized population to be unreliable. See Jennifer Van Hook and Frank D. Bean, "Estimating Unauthorized Mexican Migration to the United States: Issues and Trends," in *Binational Study: Migration Between Mexico and the United States* (Washington, DC: US Commission on Immigration Reform, 1998), pp. 538-540.

[3] Except as otherwise noted, this report focuses exclusively on border security as it relates to the prevention of unauthorized migration. On the relationship among unauthorized migration, illegal drugs and other contraband, international terrorists, and other types of border threats, see CRS Report R42969, *Border Security: Understanding Threats at U.S. Borders*, by Marc R. Rosenblum, Jerome P. Bjelopera, and Kristin Finklea.

[4] CRS Report RL33874, *Unauthorized Aliens Residing in the United States: Estimates Since 1986*, by Ruth Ellen Wasem.

[5] Ibid.

[6] United States Border Patrol (USBP), "Southwest Border Sectors: Total Apprehensions by Fiscal Year," http://cbp.gov/linkhandler/cgov/border_security/border_patrol/usbp_statistics /usbp_fy12_stats/appr_swb.ctt/ appr_swb.pdf.

[7] See for example, the White House, "Fixing the Immigration System for America's 21st Century Economy," accessed March 7, 2013, http://www.whitehouse.gov/issues

[8] See for example, Alan Gomez, "Border Security Quandary Could Kill Immigration Bill," USA Today, April 2, 2013.

[9] Act of May 28, 1924; (43 Stat. 240).

[10] Immigration Act of May 26, 1924 (43 Stat. 153).

[11] See U.S. Customs and Border Protection (CBP), "Border Patrol History," http://www.cbp.gov /xp/cgov/ border_security/border_patrol/border_patrol_ohs/history.xml.

[12] See Kitty Calavita, Inside the State: The Bracero Program, Immigration, and the I.N.S. (New York: Routledge, 1992); Mark Reisler, By the Sweat of Their Brow: Mexican Immigrant Labor in the United States, 1900-1940 (Westport, CT: Greenwood Press, 1976); Douglas S. Massey, Jorge Durand, and Nolan J. Malone, Beyond Smoke and Mirrors: Mexican Immigration in an Era of Economic Integration (New York: Russell Sage Foundation, 2002).

[13] See CRS Report R42560, Mexican Migration to the United States: Policy and Trends, coordinated by Marc R. Rosenblum. Legislative changes included the termination of the U.S.-Mexican Bracero guest worker program in 1965 and the imposition of numeric limits on migration from Mexico and other Western Hemisphere countries pursuant to the Immigration and Nationality Act Amendments of 1965 (P.L. 89-236).

[14] The IRCA also included an amnesty for certain illegal immigrants, imposed sanctions on employers who knowingly hire unauthorized immigrant workers, and revised the existing H-2 visa program to create the current H-2A and H-2B programs.

[15] The seven laws that included border-related provisions were the Immigration Act of 1990 (P.L. 101-649), the Illegal Immigration Reform and Immigrant Responsibility Act of 1996 (P.L. 104-208, Div. C), the USA-PATRIOT Act of 2002 (P.L. 107-56), the Homeland Security Act of 2002 (P.L. 107-296), the Intelligence Reform and Terrorism Prevention Act of 2004 (108-458), the REAL-ID Act of 2005 (P.L. 109-13, Div. B), and the Secure Fence Act of 2006 (P.L. 109-367). The four laws that did not include specific border-related measures were the Anti-Drug Abuse Act of 1988 (P.L. 100-690), the Personal Responsibility and Work Opportunity Reconciliation Act of 1996 (P.L. 104-93), the Antiterrorism and Effective Death Penalty Act of 1996 (P.L. 104-132), and the Immigration and Naturalization Service Data Management Improvement Act of 2000 (P.L. 106-215).

[16] U.S. Office of National Drug Control Policy, National Drug Control Strategy: Reclaiming Our Communities from Drugs and Violence (Washington, DC: U.S. Department of Justice, 1994), https://www.ncjrs.gov/pdffiles1/ondcp/ 150489.pdf.

[17] U.S. Border Patrol, Border Patrol Strategic Plan: 1994 and Beyond, July 1994, pp. 6-7 (Hereinafter, National Strategic Plan).

[18] National Strategic Plan, pp. 9-10.

[19] National Strategic Plan, pp. 10-12.

[20] National Strategic Plan, pp. 9-10.

[21] U.S. General Accounting Office, Illegal Immigration: Southwest Border Strategy Results Inconclusive; More Evaluation Needed, GAO/GGD-98-21, December 1997.

[22] U.S. Congress, Senate Committee on Appropriations, Departments of Commerce, Justice, and State, The Judiciary, and Related Agencies Appropriations Bill, 1996, report to accompany

H.R. 2076, 104th Cong., 1st sess., S.Rept. 104- 139 and U.S. Congress, House Committee on Appropriations, *Making Appropriations for the Departments of Commerce, Justice, and State, The Judiciary, and Related Agencies For the Fiscal Year Ending September 30, 1996, and for Other Purposes,* report to accompany H.R. 2076, 104th Cong., 1st sess., H.Rept. 104-378.

[23] P.L. 104-208, Div. C §102.

[24] Department of Homeland Security, Bureau of Customs and Border Protection, *National Border Patrol Strategy,* March 1, 2005. Hereinafter, *USBP National Strategy.*

[25] *USBP National Strategy,* p. 3. This definition differs from the statutory definition found in Section 2 of the Secure Fence Act of 2006 (P.L. 109-367); see in this report "Operational Control of the Border."

[26] CBP, *2012-2016 Border Patrol Strategic Plan,* Washington, DC: 2012, p. 7.

[27] Ibid.

[28] DHS, "Fact Sheet: Secure Border Initiative," https://www.hsdl.org/?view&did=440470.

[29] Ibid.

[30] Prior to 1996, the INA included distinct provisions for the "exclusion" of inadmissible aliens and the "deportation" of certain aliens from within the United States. Pursuant to §§301-309 of the Illegal Immigration Reform and Immigrant Responsibility Act of 1996 (IIRIRA, P.L. 104-208, Div. C), deportation and exclusion proceedings were combined into a unified "removal" proceeding (8 U.S.C. 1229a). This report uses "deportation" to refer to the compulsory return of aliens to their country of origin prior to the implementation of IIRIRA in 1997, and "removal" to refer to aliens returned under these provisions since 1997.

[31] DHS estimated that there were 623,292 alien "absconders" in August 2006, many of whom had failed to appear for removal hearings after being apprehended at the border; see Doris Meissner and Donald Kerwin, *DHS and Immigration: Taking Stock and Correcting Course,* Migration Policy Institute, Washington, DC, February 2009, p. 44, http://www.migration

[32] DHS, "Fact Sheet: Secure Border Initiative," https://www.hsdl.org/?view&did=440470.

[33] CBP, "DHS Secretary Announces End to 'Catch and Release' on Southern Border," http://www.cbp.gov/xp/cgov/ admin/c1_archive/messages/end_catch_release.xml.

[34] DHS, "Fact Sheet: Secure Border Initiative," https://www.hsdl.org/?view&did=440470.

[35] Ibid.

[36] Ibid. Interior enforcement programs are not discussed in this report; see CRS Report R42057, *Interior Immigration Enforcement: Programs Targeting Criminal Aliens,* by Marc R. Rosenblum and William A. Kandel; and CRS Report R40002, *Immigration-Related Worksite Enforcement: Performance Measures,* by Andorra Bruno.

[37] Prior to development of the Consequence Delivery System, most non-Mexican aliens already were placed in formal removal proceedings and, after 2005, were normally detained until a removal order was implemented (see in this report **"DHS Secure Border Initiative"**).

[38] Section 240B of the INA permits immigration agents and judges to allow certain removable aliens to "voluntarily depart" the United States. In contrast with aliens subject to formal removal, aliens subject to voluntary departure generally do not face additional immigration-related penalties.

[39] Pursuant to §§301-309 of the Illegal Immigration Reform and Immigrant Responsibility Act of 1996 (IIRIRA, P.L. 104-208, Div. C), deportation and exclusion proceedings were combined into a unified "removal" proceeding (INA §240); and immigration judges were given discretion to permit aliens who are subject to removal to "voluntarily depart" in lieu of facing formal removal proceedings (INA §240B).

[40] "Aliens" is synonymous with non-citizens, including legal permanent residents, temporary nonimmigrants, and unauthorized aliens.

[41] INA §212(a)(9).

[42] INA §276.

[43] Aliens who indicate an intention to apply for asylum or a fear of persecution are not subject to formal removal; for a fuller discussion of expedited removal see CRS Report RL33109, *Immigration Policy on Expedited Removal of Aliens*, by Alison Siskin and Ruth Ellen Wasem.

[44] Ibid. Under the 2006 policy, most Mexicans apprehended at the Southwest border were not placed in expedited removal proceedings unless they had previous criminal convictions.

[45] CBP's expanded use of reinstatement of removal depended, in part, on its ability to identify repeat offenders by enrolling their biometric data in the Automated Biometric Identification System (IDENT) system, a database of over 150 million individual records, making it the largest biometric database in the world. IDENT was implemented along the Southwest border beginning in 1999. For a fuller discussion of the US-VISIT system see archived CRS Report R42985, *Issues in Homeland Security Policy for the 113th Congress*, coordinated by William L. Painter; and CRS Report CRS Report RL32234, *U.S. Visitor and Immigrant Status Indicator Technology (US-VISIT) Program*, by Lisa Seghetti and Stephen R. Vina.

[46] Aliens apprehended at the border may face federal immigration-related criminal charges for illegal entry (8 U.S.C. §1325) or (on a second or subsequent apprehension) illegal re-entry (8 U.S.C. §1326), and in some cases they may face charges related to human smuggling (8 U.S.C. §1324) and visa and document fraud (18 U.S.C. §1546). Unlawful *presence* in the United States absent additional factors is a civil violation, not a criminal offense. See CRS Report RL32480, *Immigration Consequences of Criminal Activity*, by Michael John Garcia.

[47] A total of about 3,000 people were transferred to Mexico for prosecution under the program in FY2005-FY2012, according to data provided to CRS by CBP Office of Congressional Affairs.

[48] See U.S. Congress, House Committee on Homeland Security, Subcommittee on Border and Maritime Security, *Does Administrative Amnesty Harm our Efforts to Gain and Maintain Operational Control of the Border*, testimony of U.S. Border Patrol Chief Michael J. Fisher, 112th Cong., 1st sess., October 4, 2011.

[49] Ibid.

[50] See U.S. Congress, House Committee on Homeland Security, Subcommittee on Border and Maritime Security, *Does Administrative Amnesty Harm our Efforts to Gain and Maintain Operational Control of the Border*, testimony of U.S. Border Patrol Chief Michael J. Fisher, 112th Cong., 1st sess., October 4, 2011. Most alien smugglers reportedly charge aliens a set fee to enter the United States regardless of the number of attempts, so one goal of the high consequence enforcement programs is to disrupt smugglers' business model.

[51] Ibid. The Consequence Delivery System was formally launched January 1, 2011.

[52] Alan Bersin, *The State of US/Mexico Border Security*, Center for American Progress, August 4, 2011. Under section 240B of the Immigration and Nationality Act (INA), immigration officers and/or immigration judges may permit certain aliens to depart the United States in lieu of (or at the termination of) a formal removal hearing, a process known as "voluntary departure" or "voluntary return." Bersin indicated that certain aliens may still be eligible for voluntary return, such as aliens younger than 18 years old traveling without a parent or legal guardian (i.e., unaccompanied minors).

[53] According to CBP Office of Congressional Affairs (April 24, 2013), aliens repatriated through the Alien Transfer Exit Program (ATEP) typically are voluntarily returned or subject to

expedited removal. Thus, ATEP's high recidivism rates are partly a result of the relatively high rates associated with these two outcomes.

[54] See Figure 2 for sources. Due to the manner in which the Border Patrol collects and organizes its data, all statistics presented in this report (except where otherwise indicated) are based on the federal fiscal year, which begins October 1 and ends on September 30. All dollar amounts in this report are nominal values for the year from which data are reported, with adjustments for inflation here and below based on CRS calculations using Bureau of Labor Statistics, "CPI Inflation Calculator," http://data.bls.gov/cgi-bin/cpicalc.pl.

[55] Account-level data are from the House Explanatory Statement to accompany P.L. 113-6. Also see CRS Report R42644, *Department of Homeland Security: FY2013 Appropriations*, coordinated by William L. Painter.

[56] Ibid.

[57] Department of Homeland Security, "Secure and Manage Our Borders," http://www.dhs.gov/xabout/gc_1240606351110.shtm.

[58] Over one-third of all federal criminal cases commenced in 2009-10 were for immigration cases; see U.S. Courts, *U.S. District Courts - Criminal Cases Commenced, by Offense*, Washington, DC, 2011, http://www.uscourts.gov/ Viewer.aspx?doc=/uscourts/Statistics/FederalJudicialCaseloadStatistics/2010/tables/D02CMar10.pdf. The prosecution of these cases involves expenditures by DOJ prosecutors, federal marshals, the federal bureau of prisons, and the U.S. district and magistrate court systems, among others. The costs of border enforcement borne by federal law enforcement and judicial officials outside of DHS are difficult to describe because these agencies do not list border-specific obligations in their budget documents. Also see National Research Council Committee on Estimating Costs of Immigration Enforcement in the Department of Justice, op. cit.

[59] The Immigration Act of 1990 (P.L. 101-649) authorized an increase of 1,000 Border Patrol agents; the IIRIRA (P.L. 104-208, Div. C) authorized an increase of a total of 5,000 Border Patrol agents in FY1997-FY2001; the Uniting and Strengthening America by Providing Appropriate Tools Required to Intercept and Obstruct Terrorism Act (USA PATRIOT, P.L. 107-56) authorized INS to triple the number of Border Patrol agents at the northern border; and the Intelligence Reform and Terrorism Prevention Act (P.L. 108-458) authorized an increase of 10,000 Border Patrol agents between FY2006 and FY2010.

[60] CBP Office of Congressional Affairs, January 9, 2013.

[61] See sources cited in Figure 3.

[62] See CRS Report R41286, *Securing America's Borders: The Role of the Military*, by R. Chuck Mason.

[63] P.L. 101-510. Div. A, Title X, §1004; also see Ibid.

[64] 32 U.S.C. §§502(a) and 502(f); also see CRS Report R41286, *Securing America's Borders: The Role of the Military*, by R. Chuck Mason.

[65] See CRS Report R41286, *Securing America's Borders: The Role of the Military*, by R. Chuck Mason.

[66] Ibid.

[67] Associated Press, "National Guard Troops at Mexico Border Cut to Fewer Than 300," *USA Today*, December 20, 2011.

[68] Homeland Security Today, "Pentagon Extends Deployment of National Guard in CBP Air Support Mission," December 7, 2012.

[69] Customs and Border Protection, "Tactical Infrastructure: History and Purpose," http://www.cbp.gov/xp/cgov/ border_security/ti/about_ti/ti_history.xml.

[70] P.L. 109-367 identified five specific stretches of the border where fencing was to be installed; CBP Congressional Affairs provided CRS with this estimate of the total mileage covered by the law on September 25, 2006.

[71] P.L. 110-161, Div. E, §564. Unlike under prior law, the Consolidated Appropriations Act, as enacted, does not specify that reinforced fencing be "at least 2 layers." See P.L. 104-208, Div. C, §102(b), as amended by P.L. 109-367, §3.

[72] P.L. 110-161, Div. E, §564.

[73] Testimony of DHS Secretary Janet Napolitano before the Senate Judiciary Committee, *The Border Security, Economic Opportunity, and Immigration Modernization Act, S. 744*, 113th Cong., 1st sess., April 23, 2013.

[74] See, for example, testimony of DHS Inspector General Richard L. Skinner before the House Homeland Security Committee, Subcommittee on Management, Integration, and Oversight, *New Secure Border Initiative*, 109th Cong., 1st sess., December 16, 2005; GAO, *Secure Border Initiative: DHS Needs to Address Significant Risks in Delivering Key Technology Investment*, GAO-08-1086, September 22, 2008; and GAO, Secure *Border Initiative: Technology Deployment Delays Persist and the Impact of Border Fencing Has Not Been Assessed*, GAO-09-896, http://www.gao.gov/new.items/d09896.pdf.

[75] See DHS Inspector General (DHS IG), *Secure Border Initiative: DHS Needs to Address Significant Risks in Delivering Key Technology Investment*, DHS OIG-09-80, Washington, DC, June 2009; DHS IG, *Controls Over SBInet Program Cost and Schedule Could Be Improved*, DHS OIG-10-96, Washington, DC, June 2010.

[76] Testimony of CBP Assistant Commissioner Mark Borkowski before the House Committee on Homeland Security, Subcommittee on Border and Maritime Security, *After SBInet–The Future of Technology on the Border*, 112th Cong., 1st sess., March 15, 2011.

[77] DHS, *Report on the Assessment of the Secure Border Initiative Network (SBInet) Program*, Washington, DC, 2010, p. 1.

[78] 2012 data from U.S. Border Patrol Office of Congressional Affairs November 8, 2012; FY2006 data from DHS Congressional Budget Justification 2006; 2005 data from GAO, "Border Security: Key Unresolved Issues Justify Reevaluation of Border Surveillance Technology Program," GAO-06-295, February 2006.

[79] CBP Office of Congressional Affairs, December 12, 2012.

[80] U.S. Congress, Senate Committee on the Judiciary, *The Future of Drones in America: Law Enforcement and Privacy Considerations*, testimony of DHS Acting Officer for Civil Rights and Civil Liberties Tamara Kessler, 113th Congress, 1st sess., March 20, 2013.

[81] CBP Office of Congressional Affairs, March 19, 2013.

[82] Ibid.; and CBP Office of Air and Marine, 2011 Air and Marine Milestones and Achievements," http://www.cbp.gov/ xp/cgov/border_security/am/operations/2011_achiev.xml

[83] Northern border UAS are based in Grand Forks, ND; Southwest border UAS are based in Sierra Vista, AZ (four systems) and Corpus Christi, TX (one system); and maritime UAS are based in Corpus Christi, TX (one system) and in Cape Canaveral, FL (two systems).

[84] Ibid.

[85] CBP Office of Congressional Affairs, March 21, 2013.

[86] Deportable aliens located refer to Border Patrol apprehensions and ICE administrative arrests. Prior to 1952, data refer to Border Patrol apprehensions.

[87] Also see Adam Isacson and Maureen Meyer, "Border Security and Migration: A Report from South Texas," *Washington Office on Latin America*, http://www.wola.org/sites/default/files /downloadable/Mexico/2013/ Border%20Security%20and%20Migration%20South%20Texas.pdf.

[88] Biometric data of persons apprehended are recorded in the Automated Biometric Identification System (IDENT) system. When Border Patrol agents enter aliens' biometric data in the IDENT system, the data are automatically checked against DHS' "recidivist" database, which is used to track repeat entrants, and its "lookout" database, which is used to identify criminal aliens. US-VISIT workstations also are fully interoperable with the Federal Bureau of Investigation's (FBI) 10-print Integrated Automated Fingerprint Identification System (IAFIS), a biometric database that includes data on criminal records and the Department of Defense's (DOD) Automated Biometric Identification System (ABIS), which contains national security data.

[89] These calculations are based on aggregate date provided to CRS; individual-level IDENT data could be used to calculate the median number of apprehensions per individual in the data set, which may be a more precise indicator.

[90] For a fuller discussion, see U.S. Government Accountability Office (GAO), *Border Patrol: Key Elements of Strategic Plan not Yet in Place to Inform Border Security Status and Resource Needs*, GAO-13-25, December 2012 (hereafter: GAO, *Key Elements of Strategic Plan*.) Also see Elliot Spagat, "Under Pressure, Border Patrol Now Counts Getaways," *Associate Press*, April 22, 2013.

[91] Ibid., p. 30.

[92] Mexicans accounted for about 59% of unauthorized migrants in the United States in 2011; see Michael Hoefer, Nancy Rytina, and Bryan Baker, *Estimates of the Unauthorized Immigrant Population Residing in the United States: January 2011*, Department of Homeland Security, Office of Immigration Statistics, Washington, DC, March 201. For a fuller discussion, see CRS Report R42560, *Mexican Migration to the United States: Policy and Trends*, coordinated by Marc R. Rosenblum.

[93] NRC, *Options for Estimating Illegal Entries*, pp. 5-4 – 5-15.

[94] See for example, Wayne A. Cornelius and Idean Salehyan, "Does border enforcement deter unauthorized immigration? The case of Mexican migration to the United States of America," *Regulation & Governance* 1.2 (2007): pp. 139-153; Manuela Angelucci, "U.S. Border Enforcement and the Net Flow of Mexican Illegal Migration," *Economic Development and Cultural Change*, 60, 2 (2012):311-357.

[95] CRS Calculations based on data provided by Princeton University Mexico Migration Project. All figures are based on three-year moving averages of annual apprehension probabilities.

[96] CRS calculations based on data provided by University of California-San Diego Mexico Migration Field Research Project. All figures are based on three-year moving averages of annual apprehension probabilities. Figures are based on total apprehensions divide by total trips, not once-or-more apprehension rates by individual migrants.

[97] Estimates provided by CBP Office of Congressional Affairs, April 24, 2013. Border Patrol reportedly estimates apprehensions using a methodology broadly similar to the capture-recapture method discussed elsewhere in this report (see "Estimating Illegal Flows Using Recidivism Data").

[98] Survey data on at-the-border deterrence may under-estimate deterrence rates due to the difficulty of measuring successful entry on a single trip, versus successful entry over the course of a lifetime.

[99] See Princeton University Mexican Migration Project, "Access to Border-Crossing Guides and Family/Friends on First Undocumented Trip," http://mmp.opr.princeton.edu/results/002 coyote-en.aspx.

[100] See Bryan Roberts, Gordon Hanson, and Derekh Cornwell et al., *An Analysis of Migrant Smugglng Costs along the Southwest Border*, DHS Office of Immigration Statistics,

Washington, DC, November 2010, http://www.dhs.gov/ xlibrary/assets/statistics /publications/ois-smuggling-wp.pdf. The extent to which smugglers may pass their costs along to migrants also depends on the elasticity of migration with respect to such costs, as Roberts et al. discuss; smuggling fees may also therefore depend on the broader migration context, including economic "pulls" and "pushes" in the United States and its migration partner states.

[101] All data are CRS calculations based on data provided by Princeton University Mexico Migration Project and UCSD Mexican Migration Field Research Project.

[102] See for example, U.S. Congress, House Committee on Homeland Security, Subcommittee on Borders and Maritime Security, *Measuring Outcomes to Understand the State of Border Security*, 113th Congress, 1st sess., March 20, 2013; U.S. Congress, Senate Committee on Homeland Security and Governmental Affairs, *Border Security: Measuring Progress and Addressing the Challenges,* 113th Congress, 1st sess., March 14, 2013.

[103] U.S. Congress, House Committee on Homeland Security, Subcommittee on Borders and Maritime Security, *Measuring Outcomes to Understand the State of Border Security*, testimony of Assistant Commissioner of Homeland Security Mark Borkowski, 113th Congress, 1st sess., March 20, 2013; U.S. Congress, House Committee on Homeland Security, Subcommittee on Borders and Maritime Security, *Measuring Outcomes to Understand the State of Border Security*, testimony of Border Patrol Chief Michael Fisher, 113th Congress, 1st sess., March 20, 2013. Also see U.S. Congress, House Committee on Homeland Security, Subcommittee on Border and Maritime Security, *What Does a Secure Border Look Like*, testimony by Marc R. Rosenblum, 113th Cong., 1st sess., February 26, 2013.

[104] See Edward Alden and Bryan Roberts, "Are U.S. Borders Secure? Why We Don't Know and How to Find Out," *Foreign Affairs* 90, 4 (2011): pp. 19-26.

[105] For a fuller discussion, see GAO, *Key Elements of Strategic Plan*, pp. 28-31.

[106] See for example, Andrew Becker, "New Drone Radar Reveals Border Patrol 'Gotaways' in High Numbers," *Center for Investigative Reporting*, April 4, 2013.

[107] GAO, *Key Elements of Strategic Plan*, p. 24.

[108] For a fuller discussion of border metric methodologies and additional estimates of border security, also see Bryan Roberts, John Whitley and Edward Alden, *Managing Illegal Immigration to the United States: How Effective is Enforcement?* New York: Council on Foreign Relations Press, 2013 (hereafter: Roberts et al., *Managing Illegal Immigration to the United States*).

[109] For a clear discussion of this methodology, see Jeffrey S. Passel, "The Size and Characteristics of the Unauthorized Migrant Population in the U.S.," *Pew Hispanic Center*, March 6, 2006, http://www.pewhispanic.org/2006/03/07/sizeand-characteristics-of-the-unauthorized-migrant-population-in-the-us/. Also see CRS Report RL33874, *Unauthorized Aliens Residing in the United States: Estimates Since 1986*, by Ruth Ellen Wasem.

[110] In general, unauthorized migrants enter the United States three ways: by crossing the border without inspection between ports of entry (the focus of this report); by entering illegally through ports of entry, either by using a fraudulent document or by hiding in a vehicle; or by entering legally and then overstaying a temporary visa or becoming deportable for some other reason.

[111] See Department of Justice, *FY2001 Performance Report & FY2002 Revised Final, FY2003 Performance Plan*, Washington, DC 2001, pp. 120-122.

[112] See, for example, Edward Alden and Bryan Roberts, "Are US Borders Secure? Why We Don't Know, and How to Find Out," *Foreign Affairs*, vol. 90, no. 4 (July/August 2011), pp. 19-26.

[113] U.S. Government Accountability Office, *Border Security: Preliminary Observations on Border Control Measuers for the Southwest Border*, GAO-11-374T, February 15, 2011, p. 7.

[114] Ibid., p. 8.

[115] U.S. Congress, House Committee on Homeland Security, Subcommittee on Border and Maritime Security, *Securing Our Borders: Operational Control and the Path Forward*, 112th Congress, 1st sess., February 15, 2010.

[116] DHS did not report on border miles under effective control in its FY2010 Annual Performance Report; see DHS, *Annual Performance Report: Fiscal Years 2010-2012*, Washington, DC, April 2011, http://www.dhs.gov/xlibrary/ assets/cfo_apr_fy2010.pdf.

[117] CBP Office of Congressional Affairs, March 15, 2013.

[118] U.S. Congress, House Committee on Homeland Security, Subcommittee on Borders and Maritime Security, *Measuring Outcomes to Understand the State of Border Security*, testimony of Border Patrol Chief Michael Fisher, 113th Congress, 1st sess., March 20, 2013.

[119] U.S. Congress, Senate Committee on Homeland Security and Governmental Affairs, *Securing the Border: Progress at the Federal Level*, testimony of Secretary of Homeland Security Janet Napolitano, 112th Cong., 1st sess., May 4, 2011.

[120] CBP Office of Congressional Affairs, December 9, 2011.

[121] U.S. Congress, House Committee on Homeland Security, Subcommittee on Borders and Maritime Security, *Measuring Outcomes to Understand the State of Border Security*, testimony of Assistant Commissioner of Homeland Security Mark Borkowski, 113th Congress, 1st sess., March 20, 2013.

[122] Ibid.

[123] That is, whereas using apprehensions as a metric of border security is problematic because apprehensions depend on border resources, the ratio of apprehensions to got aways is somewhat less problematic because both apprehensions *and* estimated known got aways depend on resources, so the ratio may more accurately reflect the proportion of aliens that successfully enters. Nonetheless, the ratio may still be sensitive to border resources if estimating inflows is less (or more) resource-intensive than apprehending aliens. And the enforcement rate by itself may not be an acceptable metric without also considering data on total illegal attempts: many would consider a 10% effectiveness rate based on 100 entry attempts to be more effective than a 90% rate based on a million attempts, for example.

[124] According to CBP Office of Congressional Affairs December 20, 2011 and more recent CRS conversations with DHS officials, DHS reportedly plans to use a capture-recapture model as one element of the border conditions index (BCI).

[125] Thomas J. Espenshade, "Using INS Border Apprehension Data to Measure the Flow of Undocumented Migrants Crossing the U.S.-Mexico Frontier," *International Migration Review*, vol. 29, no. 2 (Summer 1995), pp. 545-565.

[126] In statistical methods, the odds of apprehension equal the probability of apprehension divided by one minus the probability of apprehension; see Ibid.

[127] Ibid. The basic model also assumes that that the odds of being apprehended are the same across different border regions and across multiple attempts to cross the border.

[128] Mexicans accounted for 87% of USBP apprehensions in FY2010, 84% in FY2011, and 73% in FY2012, the three lowest proportions ever recorded.

[129] See Roberts et al., *Managing Illegal Immigration to the United States*); Panel on Survey Options for Estimating the Flow of Unauthorized Crossings at the U.S.-Mexico Border, *Options for Estimating Illegal Entries at the U.S.-Mexico Border*, Washington, DC: National Research Council, 2012 (hereafter: NRC, *Options for Estimating Illegal Entries*).

Accounting for deterrence, flows are estimated to be equal to the number of total apprehensions divided by the the odds of successful enforcement; and the probability of successful enforcement is defined as the number of recidivists divided by total apprehensions, divided by one minus the probability of deterrence.

[130] Princeton University Mexican Migration Project, "Probability of a Mexican Taking a First U.S. Trip," http://mmp.opr.princeton.edu/results/009firsttrip-en.aspx.

[131] Jeffrey Passel and D'Vera Cohn, "Unauthorized Immigrants: 11.1 Million in 2011," Pew Hispanic Center, December 6, 2012, http://www.pewhispanic.org/2012 /12/06 /unauthorized-immigrants-11-1-million-in-2011/; also see CRS Report RL33874, *Unauthorized Aliens Residing in the United States: Estimates Since 1986*, by Ruth Ellen Wasem.

[132] Jeffrey Passel, D'Vera Cohn and Ana Gonzalez-Barrera, "Net Migration from Mexico Falls to Zero—and Perhaps Less," Washington, DC: Pew Hispanic Center, May 3, 2012.

[133] GAO, *Key Elements of Strategic Plan*, pp. 74-82. Effectiveness rates in this paragraph are defined as the proportion of known illegal entrants who are apprehended or return to Mexico; effectiveness rates are lower if turn-backs are not counted in the numerator.

[134] As Figure 9 illustrates, the model estimates that illegal inflows reached their lowest point in 2009 if deterrence is assumed to be 40%, while inflows reached their lowest point in 2011 if deterrence is assumed to be 20%.

[135] See, for example, Douglas S. Massey, Joaquin Arango, and Graeme Hugo et al., *Worlds In Motion: Understanding International Migration at the End of the Millenium*, 2nd ed. (New York: Oxford University Press, 2005).

[136] On the effects of Mexico's falling birthrate on U.S. immigration, see Gordon H. Hanson, Esther Duflo, and Craig McIntosh, "The Demography of Mexican Migration to the United States," *American Economic Review*, vol. 99, no. 2 (May 2009), pp. 22-27. Also see CRS Report R42560, *Mexican Migration to the United States: Policy and Trends*, coordinated by Marc R. Rosenblum.

[137] Among Mexicans who migrated illegally to look for work (83% of those in the survey), 60% of those repatriated in 2010 reported that they intended to return to the United States immediately, and 80% reported that they intended to return eventually, down from 81% and 92%, respectively, in 2005. Among new unauthorized migrants (those who had spent less than a week in the United States before being repatriated to Mexico), 18% of those repatriated in 2010 reported that they would *not* return to the United States compared to 6% in 2005. See Jeffrey Passel, D'Vera Cohn, and Ana Gonzalez-Barrera, *Net Migration from Mexico Falls to Zero—And Perhaps Less*, Pew Hispanic Center, Washington, DC, 2012, http://www.pewhispanic.org/files/2012/04/PHC-04-23a-Mexican-Migration.pdf, pp. 24-25.

[138] See for example, Scott Borger, Gordon Hanson, and Bryan Roberts "The Decision to Emigrate From Mexico," presentation at the Society of Government Economists annual conference, November 6, 2012; Manuela Angelucci, "U.S. Border Enforcement and the Net Flow of Mexican Illegal Migration," *Economic Development and Cultural Change*, 60, 2 (2012):311-357; Rebecca Lessem. "Mexico-US Immigration: Effects of Wages and Border Enforcement," Carnegie Mellon University, Research Showcase, May 2, 2012.

[139] See for example, Wayne Cornelius, "Evaluating Recent US Immigration Control Policy: What Mexican Migrants Can Tell Us," in *Crossing and Controlling Borders: Immigration Policies and Their Impact on Migrants' Journeys*, ed. Mechthild Baumann, Astrid Lorenz, and Kerstin Rosenhow (Farmington, MI: Budrich Unipress Ltd, 2011); Douglas S. Massey, Jorge Durand, and Nolan J. Malone, *Beyond Smoke and Mirrors: Mexican Immigration in an Era of Economic Integration* (Russell Sage Foundation, 2002).

[140] See Manuela Angelucci, "U.S. Border Enforcement and the Net Flow of Mexican Illegal Migration," *Economic Development and Cultural Change*, 60, 2 (2012):311-357.

[141] See CRS Report R42057, *Interior Immigration Enforcement: Programs Targeting Criminal Aliens*, by Marc R. Rosenblum and William A. Kandel.

[142] See Debra A. Hoffmaster, Gerard Murphy, and Shannon McFadden et al., *Police and Immigration: How Chiefs are Leading Their Communities through the Challenges*, Police Executive Research Forum, Washington, DC, 2010, http://www.policeforum.org/library /immigration/PERFImmigrationReportMarch2011.pdf.

[143] In 2011, for example, of the 238 migrants deaths for which DHS was able to determine a cause of death, 139 were attributed to exposure to heat or cold or water-related; data provided to CRS by CBP Office of Congressional Affairs December 15, 2011.

[144] Also see Karl Eschbach, Jacqueline Hagan, and Nestor Rodriguez et al., "Death at the Border," *International Migration Review*, vol. 33, no. 2 (Summer 1999), pp. 430-454.

[145] National Strategic Plan, p. 11-12.

[146] The USBP's Border Patrol Search, Trauma, and Rescue Unit (BORSTAR) is comprised of agents with specialized skills and training for tactical medical search and rescue operations. BORSTAR agents provide rapid response to search and rescue and medical operations, including rescuing migrants in distress. According to CBP Office of Congressional Affairs (December 9, 2011), BORSTAR agents rescued 1,070 migrants in FY2011.

[147] For a fuller discussion, see CRS Report R41075, *Southwest Border Violence: Issues in Identifying and Measuring Spillover Violence*, by Kristin Finklea.

[148] See for example, Daniel Borunda, "El Paso Ranked Safest Large city in U.S. for 3rd Straight Year," *El Paso Times*, February 6, 2013, http://www.elpasotimes.com/ci_22523903/el-paso-ranked-safest-large-city-u-s.

[149] Uniform Crime Report (UCR) data provide the most information about crime rates, but they are not sufficiently fine-tuned to provide information on the diverse factors affecting such trends; see CRS Report RL34309, *How Crime in the United States Is Measured*, by Nathan James and Logan Rishard Council.

[150] See Stanley Bailey, Karl Eschbach, and Jacqueline Hagan et al., "Migrant Death on the US-Mexco Border 1985- 1996," *University of Houston Center for Immigration Research Working Paper Series*, vol. 96, no. 1 (1996); Jimenez, "Humanitarian Crisis," 2009.

[151] The Border Patrol has drawn criticism from human rights activists who claim that the agency's migrant death count understates the number of fatalities. Some contend that the Border Patrol undercounts fatalities by excluding skeletal remains, victims in car accidents, and corpses discovered by other agencies or local law enforcement officers; see , for example, Raymond Michalowski, "Border Militarization and Migrant Suffering: A Case of Transnational Social Injury," *Social Justice*, Summer 2007.

[152] Also see Adam Isacson and Maureen Meyer, "Border Security and Migration: A Report from South Texas," *Washington Office on Latin America*, http://www.wola.org/sites/default /files/downloadable/Mexico/2013/ Border%20Security%20and%20Migration%20South%20Texas.pdf.

[153] See Wayne Cornelius, "Evaluating Recent US Immigration Control Policy: What Mexican Migrants Can Tell Us," in *Crossing and Controlling Borders: Immigration Policies and Their Impact on Migrants' Journeys*, ed. Mechthild Baumann, Astrid Lorenz, and Kerstin Rosenhow (Farmington, MI: Budrich Unipress Ltd, 2011); Douglas S. Massey, Jorge Durand, and Nolan J. Malone, *Beyond Smoke and Mirrors: Mexican Immigration in an Era of Economic Integration* (Russell Sage Foundation, 2002).

[154] Whereas almost half of unauthorized aliens from Mexico who arrived in 1980 remained in the United States for less than a year, fewer than 20% of unauthorized Mexicans who entered in 2010 returned home within a year; see Mexican Migration Project, "Probability of Return within 12 Months," http://mmp.opr.princeton.edu/results/010returnpersen.aspx. Also see Jonathan Hicken, Mollie Cohen, and Jorge Narvaez, "Double Jeopardy: How U.S. Enforcement Policies Shape Tunkaseño Migration," in *Mexican Migration and the U.S. Economic Crisis*, ed. Wayne A. Cornelius, David FitzGerald, Pedro Lewin Fischer, and Leah Muse-Orlinoff (La Jolla, CA: University of California, San Diego Center for Comparative Immigration Studies, 2010), pp. 56-57. And whereas an estimated 60-90% of unauthorized migrants during the 1970s were single men, by 2008 men only accounted for an estimated 53% of unauthorized aliens, with women representing 34% and the remainder children; see Jeffrey S. Passel and D'Vera Cohn, *A Portrait of Unauthorized Immigrants in the United States*, Pew Hispanic Center, Washington, DC, April 14, 2009, p. 4, http://pewhispanic.org/files/reports/107.pdf.

[155] For example, changes in U.S. labor markets have resulted in more permanent (non-seasonal) employment opportunities for unauthorized aliens as well as more employment opportunities for unauthorized women; See CRS Report R41592, *The U.S. Foreign-Born Population: Trends and Selected Characteristics*, by William A. Kandel.

[156] Half of the Mexico-based family members of unauthorized aliens interviewed by the UC, San Diego MMFRP in 2009 indicated that they had a relative who had remained in the United States longer than they had intended because they feared they would be unable to reenter the United States if they returned home; see Hicken et al. "Double Jeopardy," 57-58.

[157] Hicken et al., "Double Jeopardy," pp. 60-61.

[158] Probability of apprehension on an alien's most recent attempt to illegally pass through a port of entry was 0.36, compared to 0.73 on the most recent entry attempt between ports of entry; UC San Diego MMFRP data provided to CRS September 23, 2010.

[159] CBP Office of Congressional Affairs March 21, 2013.

[160] See for example, Adolfo Flores and Ruben Vives, "New Panga Incident Investigated as Possible Smuggling Operation," *Los Angeles Times*, December 10, 2012; Dave Graham, "By Land or by Sea, Tougher U.S. Border Tests Illegal Immigrants," *Reuters*, March 20, 2013. Border tunnels are mainly used to smuggle narcotics into the United States, rather than for illegal migration.

[161] Department of Homeland Security, *Environmental Impact Statement for the Completion of the 14-mile Border Infrastructure System, San Diego, California* (July 2003), pp. 1-11.

[162] According to the GAO, about 25% of the northern border and 43% of the Southwest border consist of federal and tribal lands overseen by the U.S. Forest Service and Department of the Interior; see CRS Report R42346, *Federal Land Ownership: Overview and Data*, by Carol Hardy Vincent, Laura A. Hanson, and Marc R. Rosenblum.

[163] See for example, University of Texas School of Law, "The Texas-Mexico Border Wall," http://www.utexas.edu/ law/centers/humanrights/borderwall/.

[164] See CRS Report R42053, *Fiscal Impacts of the Foreign-Born Population*, by William A. Kandel. Although the overall economic effects of migration—and unauthorized migration in particular—are difficult to estimate, research suggests that fiscal costs of migration are disproportionately borne at the local level.

[165] See, for example, Mark Harrison, "Beefed Up Border Patrol Jolts Farmers, Cows," *Seattle Times*, November 13, 2011; Rafael Carranza, "Leaders Blame Lost Business Deals on Border Fence," *KGBT Channel 4 News*, November 2, 2009, http://www.valleycentral.com /news/story.aspx?id=371266#.Tt0oAmNM8rs Also see U.S. Chamber of Commerce, *Steps*

to a 21st Century U.S.-Mexico Border, http://www.uschamber.com/sites /default /files/reports/ 2011_us_mexico_report.pdf.

[166] See, for example, Associated Press, "Quebec-Vermont Border Communities Divided by Post-9/11 Security," CBC News: Canada, August 14, 2011.

[167] See, for example, NY School of Law, NY Civil Liberties Union, and Families for Freedom, Justice Derailed: What Raids On New York's Trains And Buses Reveal About Border Patrol's Interior Enforcement Practices, New York: November, 2011, http://www.nyclu.org/publications/report-justice-derailed-what-raids-trains-and-buses-reveal-aboutborder-patrols-interi; Lornet Turnbull and Roberto Daza, "Climate of Fear Grips Forks Illegal Immigrants," Seattle Times, June 26, 2011.

[168] See for example, American Civil Liberties Union, "Immigration Reform Should Eliminate Operation Streamline," http://www.aclu.org/files/assets/operation_streamline_issue_brief.pdf.

[169] See for example, Alan Gomez, "Lawsuits Allege abuses by Border Patrol Agents," USA Today, March 13, 2013; Judith Greene and Alexis Mazón, "Privately Operated Federal Prisons for Immigrants: Expensive, Unsafe, Unenecessary," Justice Strategies, September 13, 2012; No More Deaths/No Mas Muertes, A Culture of Cruelty: Abuse and Impunity in Short-Term U.S. Border Patrol Custody, 2011.

[170] See, for example, National Immigration Forum, Operation Streamline: Unproven Benefits Outweighed by Costs to Taxpayers, Washington, DC, September 2012.

[171] Thomas H. Cohen, Special Report: Pretrial Detention and Misconduct in Federal District Courts, 1995-2010, U.S. Department of Justice, Bureau of Justice Statistics, NCJ 239673, Washington, DC, February 2013.

[172] Mark Motivans, Immigration Offenders in the Federal Justice System, 2010, U.S. Department of Justice, Bureau of Justice Statistics, NCJ 238581, Washington, DC, July 2012.

[173] Administrative Office of the U.S. Courts, Report on the Impact on the Judiciary of Law Enforcement Activities Along the Southwest Border, Washington, DC: Administrative Office of the U.S. Courts, July 2008.

[174] DHS, "Beyond the Border Action Plan," December 2011, http://www.dhs.gov/files /publications/beyond-the-borderaction-plan.shtm; also see CRS Report 96-397, Canada-U.S. Relations, coordinated by Carl Ek and Ian F. Fergusson.

[175] See for example, Dana Gabriel, "Toward a North American Police State and Security Perimeter: U.S.-Canada 'Beyond the Border Agreement,'" Global Research, May 14, 2012.

[176] See CRS Report R41349, U.S.-Mexican Security Cooperation: The Mérida Initiative and Beyond , by Clare Ribando Seelke and Kristin Finklea

[177] See CRS Report R42560, Mexican Migration to the United States: Policy and Trends, coordinated by Marc R. Rosenblum; Marc R. Rosenblum, Obstacles and Opportunities for Regional Cooperation: The US-Mexico Case, Migration Policy Institute, April 2011, http://www.migrationpolicy.org/pubs/USMexico-cooperation.pdf.

[178] Thomas J. Espenshade, "Using INS Border Apprehension Data to Measure the Flow of Undocumented Migrants Crossing the U.S.-Mexico Frontier," International Migration Review, vol. 29, no. 2 (Summer 1995), pp. 545-565.

[179] Ibid., pp. 549-550.

[180] CRS analysis of apprehensions data from DHS, Yearbook of Immigration Statistics FY2011, Washington, DC: DHS, 2012. Mexicans accounted for 90% of all apprehensions in 2000-2009, before falling to 83% in 2010 and 76% in FY2011. (Mexicans represent a lower proportion of all apprehensions than of Border Patrol apprehensions; total apprehensions data for FY2012 were not available when this report was released.)

[181] Espenshade, "Using INS Border Apprehension Data," pp. 551-552.

[182] Ibid., p. 554.

[183] The Consequence Delivery System seeks to reduce recidivism by increasing the proportion of aliens subject to formal removal, criminal charges, and/or remote repatriation (see "CBP Consequence Delivery System"). And unauthorized aliens from countries other than Mexico (i.e., 73% of USBP apprehensions in FY2012) typically are deported to their home countries, substantially raising the cost of re-entry.

[184] Roberts et al., *Managing Illegal Immigration to the United States*.

[185] CBP Office of Congressional Affairs, December 20, 2011.

[186] DHS also reportedly restricts its recidivism analysis to Mexican aliens, but may uses country-specific recidivism data to calculate apprehension rates, and may therefore estimate a somewhat lower probability of successful enforcement based on this methodology.

INDEX

#

20th century, 50, 52
9/11, 4, 6, 7, 14, 28, 37, 40, 41, 42, 44, 53, 61, 63, 89, 104
9/11 Commission, 6, 40, 41, 42

A

abuse, 88
accounting, 5, 61, 84, 87, 89
acquisitions, 68
administrative support, 64
agencies, 9, 10, 13, 14, 40, 54, 63, 90, 96, 102
air carriers, 13, 15, 29, 32, 46
air passenger screening, 43
airports, 13, 14, 15, 17, 21, 23, 28, 29, 35, 39, 41, 43, 45
Al Qaeda, 4
American Civil Liberties Union, 84, 104
annual rate, 18
appropriations, ix, 36, 37, 38, 50, 51, 52, 61, 62, 63, 65, 66, 83
Appropriations Act, 48
Appropriations Committee, 48
arrest(s), 4, 6, 19, 20, 27, 47, 53, 88, 97
ASI, 67
Asia, 41
assessment, 67, 78

assets, 55, 61, 67, 68, 89, 99, 100, 104
asylum, 95
Attorney General, 6, 7, 38, 39
Austria, 42
authority, vii, 4, 6, 13, 14, 63
automate, 26

B

bail, 55
ban, 41
banks, 44
barriers, 53, 65, 66, 87, 89
Belgium, 42
benefits, ix, 5, 10, 12, 22, 23, 38, 47, 50, 51, 83, 87, 90
bias, 21
biometric system, viii, 2, 3
birds, 87
border control, 51, 52, 56
border crossing, 29, 43, 73, 83, 85, 86
border security, ix, 5, 35, 36, 49, 50, 51, 55, 61, 63, 72, 73, 76, 77, 78, 79, 80, 83, 89, 90, 92, 99, 100
Bureau of Customs and Border Protection, viii, 49, 62, 66, 94
Bureau of Justice Statistics, 104
Bureau of Labor Statistics, 75, 96
business model, 95
business travelers, 45

businesses, ix, 10, 50

C

car accidents, 102
Caribbean, 8, 42
cash, 84
certification, 9
chain of command, 54
challenges, vii, 4, 26, 31, 37, 44, 72, 73
Chamber of Commerce, 103
children, 43, 103
city(s), 13, 43, 84
citizens, vii, 1, 2, 5, 6, 8, 10, 14, 22, 29, 31,
    33, 42, 45, 59, 89
citizenship, 9, 24, 41
civil liberties, 5
civil rights, 87, 89
classes, 4, 15, 68
clients, 48, 75
cocaine, 41
coding, 79
collaboration, 33
commerce, 5, 7
commercial, 12, 21, 41, 48, 87
communication, 43, 47
community(s), ix, 10, 50, 52, 54, 73, 83, 87,
    86, 89
competitive advantage, 15
complexity, 3
compliance, 30, 32
computer, 67
conference, 101
Congress, vii, 1, 2, 3, 4, 5, 7, 12, 15, 22, 33,
    34, 35, 36, 37, 38, 40, 43, 44, 46, 47, 50,
    51, 52, 53, 61, 63, 65, 76, 79, 88, 89, 90,
    93, 95, 97, 99, 100
consensus, 5
Consolidated Appropriations Act, 65, 97
construction, 53, 65, 66, 87, 88
Consumer Price Index, 75
containers, 21
conversations, 100
cooperation, 63, 104
cost, 31, 34, 35, 47, 67, 105

counterterrorism, 63
country of origin, 94
CPI, 75, 96
crimes, 10, 19, 41, 88
criminal activity, 84
criminality, 84
criminals, 4, 5, 41
criticism, 67, 102
CT, 93
Cuba, 8
currency, 25, 26
Customs and Border Protection, vii, 1, 3,
    40, 42, 44, 47, 48, 93, 96
Customs Service, 20, 42, 62, 64, 66
Czech Republic, 42

D

danger, 4
data collection, 26, 28, 29, 30, 31, 33, 34,
    35, 77
data set, 98
database, 9, 10, 14, 27, 28, 32, 40, 45, 67,
    89, 95, 98
deaths, ix, 50, 83, 84, 85, 88, 102
defendants, 57, 88
deficiency, 19
demographic change, 82
demographic characteristics, 84
Denmark, 42
Department of Commerce, 52
Department of Defense, 63, 65, 68, 98
Department of Homeland Security, vii, viii,
    1, 3, 27, 42, 45, 46, 48, 49, 55, 94, 96,
    98, 103
Department of Justice, 7, 41, 45, 52, 57, 78,
    93, 96, 99, 104
Department of Labor, 52
Department of the Interior, 103
deportation, vii, 4, 15, 92, 94
detection, 76, 90
detention, 55, 57, 88
deterrence, ix, 49, 53, 71, 74, 77, 81, 85, 89,
    92, 98, 101
digital cameras, 27

diminishing returns, 89
distress, 102
distribution, 5
Doha, 43
DOJ, 7, 40, 57, 62, 96
donations, 37
drug flow, 4, 25
drug smuggling, 53
drug trafficking, 14, 25
drugs, 25, 54, 92

E

economic activity, 87
economic change, 52
economic competitiveness, 32, 88
economic downturn, ix, 16, 50, 69, 75, 82
ecosystems, ix, 50, 87
education, 84
employers, 93
employment, 24, 52, 83, 103
employment opportunities, 52, 103
endangered, 87
endangered species, 87
engineering, 64
enrollment, 31
entry-exit system, viii, 2, 3, 7, 12, 26, 27, 28, 32, 33, 34, 35, 38, 39, 40
environment, 86, 87, 89
environmental impact, 83
equipment, 63, 68
erosion, 87
espionage, 4
Estonia, 42
European Union, 29
evidence, ix, 24, 50, 51, 83, 85, 86, 89
examinations, 9
exclusion, vii, 4, 94
exercise, 19
expenditures, 96
exports, 25
exposure, 84, 102

F

families, 86
family members, 103
fear, 19, 84, 95
Federal Bureau of Investigation (FBI), 10, 28, 45, 46, 84, 95, 98
federal courts, 88
Federal Government, 44
federal law, 4, 96
Federal Register, 42, 43, 45
fencing, ix, 50, 53, 55, 65, 66, 82, 87, 88, 89, 97
financial, 24
financial support, 24
fingerprints, viii, 2, 10, 14, 16, 23, 27, 28, 45, 71
Finland, 42
flight, 14, 31, 32, 68
flights, 9, 10, 12, 13, 30, 31, 32
foreign nationals, 3, 8, 40, 42
foreign-born population, 78
formation, 61
formula, 91
France, 42
fraud, 9, 28, 84, 95
funding, 15, 31, 35, 37, 52, 61, 62, 63, 66, 88
funds, 66

G

General Accounting Office (GAO), 22, 30, 33, 37, 44, 45, 46, 47, 48, 53, 81, 93, 97, 98, 99, 100, 101, 103
geography, 5
Germany, 42
governments, 14
gravity, 5
Great Depression, 50
Greece, 42
gross domestic product, 5
growth, 37, 61, 76
growth rate, 76

guardian, 95
guidance, 77
guilty, 57
Gulf Coast, 53
Gulf of Mexico, 68

H

health, 9
hemisphere, 7
heroin, 41
higher-risk travelers, viii, 2, 6
history, viii, 2, 3, 9, 29, 51, 67, 93, 96
Homeland Security Act, 6, 42, 93
host, 13, 14
House, 15, 35, 36, 37, 43, 44, 46, 47, 48, 53,
    94, 95, 96, 97, 99, 100
human, 55, 64, 75, 89, 90, 95, 102
human right(s), 89, 102
Hungary, 42

I

Iceland, 42
ID, 23, 24, 93
ideal, 58
identification, 27, 42, 64
identity, 27, 28, 39, 42
images, 67
immigrants, 14, 21, 35, 36, 53, 93, 101
Immigration Act, 41, 93, 96
Immigration and Customs Enforcement
    (ICE), 9, 10, 33, 37, 42, 45, 47, 48, 55,
    59, 63, 97
Immigration and Nationality Act, 41, 56,
    93, 95
Impact Assessment, 10, 42, 43, 45, 46
imports, 40, 41, 52
improvements, 37
inadmissible, vii, 1, 3, 8, 9, 10, 14, 15, 18,
    19, 22, 37, 41, 56, 94
individuals, 10, 19, 33, 39, 40, 71, 72, 76,
    77
inferences, 22

inflation, 61, 66, 75, 76, 96
information sharing, viii, 2, 29, 33, 34, 88
infrastructure, viii, ix, 2, 26, 29, 30, 35, 36,
    47, 49, 50, 53, 55, 61, 65, 66, 87, 89
initiation, 71
INS, 26, 28, 44, 52, 53, 62, 65, 66, 67, 96,
    100, 104, 105
inspections, vii, 1, 2, 3, 4, 5, 6, 16, 17, 18,
    20, 21, 22, 23, 26, 28, 36, 38, 40, 42, 43,
    47, 62, 66
inspectors, 4, 8
integration, 28, 45, 54
intelligence, 10, 13, 54, 64
Intelligence Reform and Terrorism
    Prevention Act, 7, 40, 93, 96
interface, 39
international law, 10
investments, ix, 50, 89, 90
Ireland, 14, 23, 42
islands, 8, 42
issues, vii, 3, 4, 23, 37, 51, 79, 89, 93
Italy, 42

J

Japan, 42
Judiciary Committee, 35, 97

L

land travelers, vii, 1, 2, 14, 16, 27
landscape, 3, 54
Latin America, 97, 102
Latvia, 42
law enforcement, 9, 10, 13, 14, 39, 44, 63,
    83, 84, 88, 90, 102
lawful travelers, vii, 1, 3, 5
laws, 4, 6, 50, 52, 63, 93
LEA, 63
lead, viii, 9, 49
legal protection, 88
legislation, 7, 36, 38, 41
legitimate travelers, vii, 4
lifetime, 98

light, 36, 66, 85, 89, 92
Lithuania, 42
low risk, 22

M

majority, vii, 1, 3, 18, 29, 34, 52, 75
management, viii, 2, 5, 38
marijuana, 4, 41
media, 77, 84
median, 98
medical, 84, 102
membership, 24, 25, 38
messages, 94
methodology, 22, 78, 80, 81, 82, 90, 91, 98, 99, 105
metropolitan areas, 84
Mexico, ix, 13, 23, 25, 35, 36, 43, 45, 50, 51, 52, 56, 57, 60, 72, 73, 75, 76, 80, 81, 82, 83, 84, 86, 88, 91, 92, 93, 95, 96, 97, 98, 99, 100, 101, 102, 103, 104, 105
Miami, 48
migrants, ix, 5, 6, 36, 50, 51, 52, 58, 73, 74, 75, 76, 77, 78, 80, 81, 82, 84, 86, 87, 89, 90, 91, 98, 99, 101, 102, 103
migration, viii, 2, 21, 33, 36, 49, 50, 51, 52, 55, 61, 69, 73, 76, 77, 81, 82, 83, 85, 86, 87, 89, 90, 92, 93, 94, 98, 99, 103
military, 42, 64, 68
minors, 89, 95
mission, vii, 1, 2, 3, 47
MMP, 73, 75
mobile device, 29
modifications, 36
morale, 37
mortality, 83, 84

N

NAFTA, 42
narcotics, 78, 90, 103
National Counterterrorism Center (NCTC), 9
National Crime Information Center, 10

National Defense Authorization Act, 63
National Drug Control Strategy, 93
National Drug Intelligence Center, 41
national origin, 41
National Research Council, 57, 73, 96, 100
national security, 7, 10, 13, 23, 28, 33, 39, 54, 98
national strategy, 76, 94
nationality, 22, 27
Netherlands, 42
New Zealand, 42
non-citizens, vii, 1, 2, 4, 14, 29, 40, 95
North America, 104
northern border, viii, 2, 5, 30, 33, 52, 63, 96, 103
Norway, 42
NRC, 73, 98, 100

O

Obama, 37, 48, 51
Obama Administration, 37, 48, 51
obstacles, 38
offenders, 88, 95
Office of National Drug Control Policy, 53, 93
officials, 10, 32, 39, 44, 57, 68, 76, 79, 84, 92, 96, 100
operating costs, 12
operations, 15, 21, 25, 26, 37, 47, 52, 55, 63, 64, 65, 68, 88, 97, 102
opportunities, 52, 68, 103
organ, 96
oversight, 30, 67
overtime, 37
ownership, 68

P

Pacific, 41, 65
Panama, 13, 43
pathways, 86
penalties, ix, 18, 19, 43, 49, 94
Pentagon, 96

permission, 8
permit, 8, 18, 22, 28, 44, 46, 56, 94, 95
photographs, viii, 2, 9, 10, 14, 27, 71
platform, 13
pleasure, 12, 40, 43
POEs, vii, 1, 2, 3, 4, 5, 6, 8, 9, 10, 14, 16,
    17, 18, 19, 20, 21, 22, 23, 27, 28, 30, 31,
    32, 34, 35, 36, 37, 38, 39, 41, 43, 44, 45,
    47, 48
police, 84
policy, vii, 4, 20, 43, 55, 78, 85, 89, 90, 95
population, 4, 51, 78, 81, 90, 91, 92, 99
port(s) of entry, vii, 1, 2, 3, 6, 9, 10, 13, 14,
    15, 19, 20, 28, 29, 30, 35, 36, 41, 42, 43,
    48, 54, 55, 56, 57, 78, 79, 81, 86, 88, 92,
    99, 103
Portugal, 42
president, 4, 6, 32, 44, 64, 88
President Obama, 32, 64, 88
prevention, ix, 49, 53, 71, 78, 84, 85, 92
prisons, 96
private sector, 37
probability, 54, 65, 73, 74, 80, 86, 91, 92,
    100, 101, 105
project, 30, 67
protection, 84, 89
public policy, 56
public safety, 33, 79, 84
public-private partnerships, 37
Puerto Rico, 23

Q

quality of life, ix, 50, 54, 79, 89
quotas, 41

R

random assignment, 21
reading, 27
real time, 68
recession, 82
recidivism, ix, 50, 59, 60, 61, 69, 71, 72, 77,
    80, 81, 82, 89, 90, 91, 92, 96, 105

recidivism rate, 59, 60, 61, 71, 72, 80, 82,
    91, 92, 96
recommendations, 13, 37, 43
reform(s), viii, 2, 7, 22, 36, 38, 39, 40, 41,
    47, 51, 52, 53, 65, 90, 92, 93, 94, 104
regulations, 6
relief, 18, 19
requirements, 3, 6, 7, 12, 23, 30, 31, 32, 39,
    41, 42, 45, 63
researchers, 77, 86, 92
resolution, 57
resources, ix, 22, 26, 36, 37, 50, 51, 54, 58,
    65, 68, 72, 77, 79, 80, 83, 84, 87, 88, 89,
    90, 100
response, 3, 5, 10, 19, 51, 52, 55, 67, 102
restrictions, 50, 52
risk(s), viii, 2, 5, 8, 9, 10, 12, 13, 22, 33, 37,
    48, 54, 68, 84
risk management, viii, 2, 5, 37, 48
routes, 5, 53, 86
rule of law, 87
rules, vii, 3, 4, 13
Russia, 46
RVS, 55, 67

S

safety, 8, 37
sanctions, 18, 93
scaling, 31
schedule delays, 67
school, 87
science, 73, 86
scope, viii, 2, 3, 40
seaports, viii, 2, 17, 29, 39, 45
Secretary of Homeland Security, 43, 65, 100
security, ix, 4, 8, 9, 12, 15, 22, 26, 28, 31,
    32, 38, 40, 47, 51, 54, 55, 63, 76, 79, 88,
    90, 93, 96, 97
seizure, 25
Senate, 46, 47, 48, 53, 93, 97, 99, 100
Senate Committee on the Judiciary, 47, 97
sensors, 55, 65, 66, 67, 68
September 11, 43
services, 37, 41

shelter, 87
shortage, 88
Singapore, 42
skeletal remains, 102
Slovakia, 42
smuggling, ix, 19, 44, 49, 53, 55, 57, 65, 75, 76, 84, 95, 99, 103
South Korea, 22, 42
southern border, viii, 2, 5, 34, 55, 90
Southwest border, ix, 44, 48, 50, 51, 52, 53, 57, 58, 59, 63, 64, 65, 68, 69, 71, 72, 73, 79, 84, 88, 89, 92, 95, 97, 103
sovereignty, vii, 4
Spain, 42
staffing, 29, 30, 31, 37, 48, 51, 55, 63
state(s), vii, ix, 4, 10, 13, 14, 19, 24, 29, 42, 50, 51, 54, 55, 63, 69, 76, 99
statistics, 51, 93, 96, 99
stock, 51, 78
structure, 54
style, 55
Supreme Court, vii, 4
surveillance, ix, 49, 50, 53, 54, 55, 61, 64, 65, 67, 68, 87, 89, 90
Sweden, 42
Switzerland, 42

T

tactics, 25
Taiwan, 42
target, 54, 88
teams, 47
technology(s), ix, 7, 29, 30, 31, 39, 44, 47, 49, 50, 53, 54, 55, 61, 65, 66, 67, 68
tension, vii, 1, 3, 4, 5, 40, 88
territory, 42
terrorism, 4, 78
terrorist attack, ix, 5, 49
terrorist watchlist, 13, 32
terrorists, 5, 8, 10, 37, 54, 65, 78, 92
testing, 31
threats, 3, 4, 5, 14, 41, 54, 79, 92
tourism, 5, 12, 41, 45
tracks, 59

trade, 25, 38, 47, 48
trafficking, 52, 54, 64, 90
training, 9, 47, 102
transmission, 45
Transportation Security Administration, 30
transshipment, 25
travel programs, viii, 2
Treasury, 44
tribal lands, 103
triggers, 35

U

U.S. Department of Commerce, 48
U.S. economy, 5
U.S. immigration law, vii, 4
U.S. immigration system, viii, 2, 3
U.S. labor market, 103
unauthorized aliens, ix, 40, 49, 76, 78, 84, 86, 90, 91, 92, 95, 103, 105
underwriting, 37
United Kingdom, 43
United Nations, 15
unlawful entries, vii, 4, 78
urban, 38
urban areas, 38
USA, 28, 39, 93, 96, 104
USA PATRIOT Act, 28, 39

V

vegetation, 87
vehicles, 10, 20, 21, 23, 37, 41
vessels, 10, 20, 68
victims, 84, 102
violence, ix, 25, 50, 83, 84, 86
violent crime, 84
Visa Waiver Program, 3, 6, 7, 8, 9, 10, 12, 39, 40, 43
visions, 32, 88

W

waiver, 14, 20

Washington, 41, 44, 46, 47, 48, 57, 92, 93, 94, 96, 97, 98, 99, 100, 101, 102, 103, 104
watches, 45
water, 102
weapons, 15, 25, 54, 90
weapons of mass destruction, 90

White House, 93
wildlife, 87, 89
withdrawal, 18
WMD, 90
workers, 31, 46, 51, 92, 93
World Bank, 41
World War I, 50, 52